THE INDIANS
and the
CALIFORNIA MISSIONS

by
Linda Lyngheim

Illustrated by
Phyllis Garber

Langtry Publications
Van Nuys, California

To my parents, husband, and friends who visited the missions with me.

Library of Congress Catalog No. 84-80543

LANGTRY PUBLICATIONS
20755 Marilla Street
Chatsworth, CA 91311

Acknowledgements: Photographs on pages: 52, 82, 87 (top), 124, 129 (top), 136, and 139 are credited to the California State Library. All other photographs are credited to Linda Lyngheim. Line drawings are created by the illustrator, Phyllis Garber except for those by Graphic Products Corporation on pages 51 and 123.

ISBN 0-915369-00-1 paper

ISBN 0-915369-04-4 hardcover

Printed in the United States of America

CALIFORNIA JUNIOR HERITAGE SERIES

The Indians and the California Missions

Father Junipero Serra the Traveling Missionary

Gold Rush Adventure

California Mission Projects & Activities

Available from:
Langtry Publications
20755 Marilla Street
Chatsworth, CA 91311

PREFACE

As an author and former children's librarian, I have realized the need for more books about California history written on a juvenile level. Through this need and my own interest in local history, I am writing this revised edition. Many years of research, revisiting missions, and additional information have gone into this new edition. Indian life before the Spaniards, mission life, and updated chapters on the missions are expanded.

My hope is that those who read it will find it useful in bringing alive the mission days in California history.

CONTENTS

THE CALIFORNIA MISSIONS

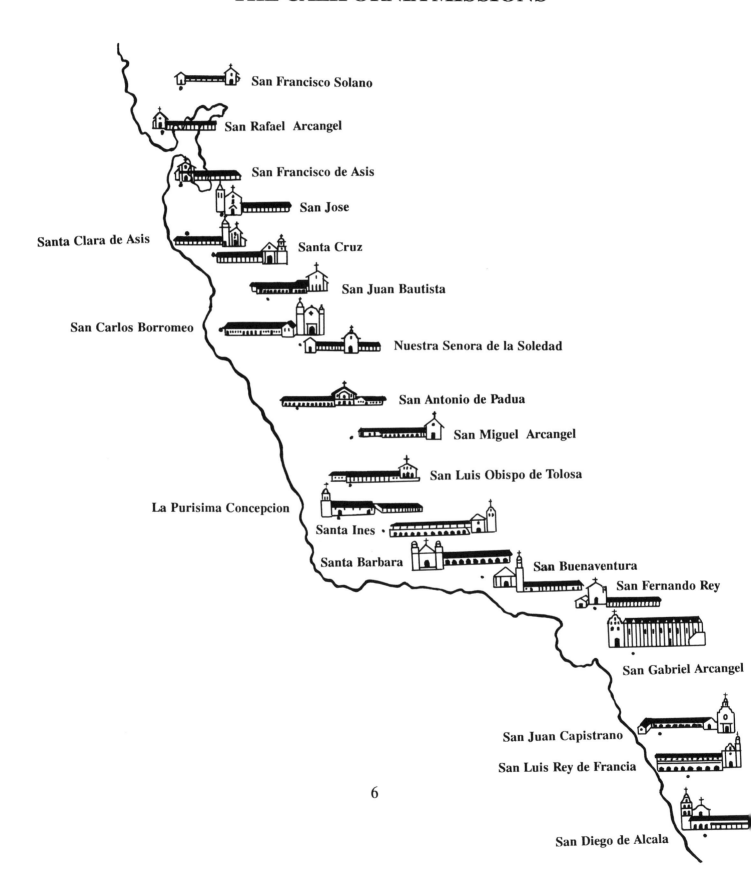

San Francisco Solano

San Rafael Arcangel

San Francisco de Asis

San Jose

Santa Clara de Asis

Santa Cruz

San Juan Bautista

San Carlos Borromeo

Nuestra Senora de la Soledad

San Antonio de Padua

San Miguel Arcangel

San Luis Obispo de Tolosa

La Purisima Concepcion

Santa Ines

Santa Barbara

San Buenaventura

San Fernando Rey

San Gabriel Arcangel

San Juan Capistrano

San Luis Rey de Francia

San Diego de Alcala

THE INDIANS
and the
CALIFORNIA MISSIONS

THE WORLD

NORTH AMERICA

California

Baja California

Mexico

ATLANTIC OCEAN

PACIFIC OCEAN

SOUTH AMERICA

EUROPE

AFRICA

CHAPTER 1

DISCOVERY OF CALIFORNIA

During the 16th century, Spain and other European countries were exploring the world looking for new lands to own. At that time an explorer named Juan Cabrillo sailed from Spain to San Diego, California. He claimed the land for his country in the year 1542.

Sir Francis Drake, an English explorer, landed off the coast of California in 1579. He claimed California for England.

In 1602 the Spanish government sent Sebastian Vizcaino to investigate pirates attacking Spanish ships in this area. While he was there, the explorer discovered Monterey Bay. He claimed the land once again for Spain.

For a long time no one seemed interested in the faraway place that is today's California. Russian fur trappers and traders had established a large trading post in northern California at Fort Ross. They sold many animal furs. Spain grew fearful that Russia would take California away from them. Spain already owned Mexico and had established missions and colonies there.

In 1768, King Charles III of Spain decided on a plan. He chose Jose de Galvez to be visitor-general or ruler to govern Mexico (New Spain). Galvez would carry out the king's orders to colonize and settle California. Portola would lead the expedition and serve as governor of the colony. A group of soldiers, explorers, Christian Indians, and missionary padres would set up missions in California. There would be twenty-one missions built along the coast of California. Each would be spaced a day's journey from the next one. First they would establish one in San Diego then a second mission at Monterey.

Galvez chose Captain Don Gaspar de Portola to lead the military part of the expedition. Father Junipero Serra, a Franciscan missionary, would be the church President. He would now be put in charge of establishing the missions in California. Under this plan, the padres would interest the native Indians in becoming Christians. The Indians would help run the missions, taking them over in time.

Along with the missions, the Spaniards would build *presidios* or forts for soldiers to guard the land and people. *Pueblos* or towns would be built where colonies of families from Mexico would settle.

To Spain this was an easy way to claim California peacefully. More than two hundred years had passed since the Spaniards had first landed here. This time they came to settle California.

CHAPTER 2

SPANISH SETTLEMENT

Sea Expeditions To California

Governor Jose de Galvez organized three sea and two land expeditions to leave from Baja, California (Mexico), for California. The people from both expeditions would meet in San Diego.

The sea expeditions would need ships for the journey. The only ships they were able to find were leaky and in poor condition. After much time was spent on repairs, the sailors loaded the ships with supplies.

What did they take with them? Sailors hauled aboard sacks of corn, wheat, peas, and wine. They filled barrels with water, dried beef, and boxes of chocolate. Tools for farming were carried on like axes, hoes, and spades. Father Serra checked to be sure the church goods were safely packed away. Altars, bells, candles, and priests' robes would be needed for the churches of the new missions. All these items would be used for the voyage and life in the new land.

During the months of January and February of 1769, the ships the *San Antonio, San Carlos,* and *San Jose* sailed from La Paz for San Diego.

Land Expeditions To California

The two land expeditions were made ready. The following month, the first land expedition departed from Santa Maria led by Captain Fernando Rivera. With him traveled Father Crespi, twenty-five soldiers, a few muleteers, and forty-two Christian Indians.

Father Serra watched them, eager to begin his journey. After serving many years as President of the Baja California missions, he looked forward to establishing new missions in California. In May he joined the second expedition commanded by Captain Don Gaspar de Portola.

What was it like to travel on an expedition? The day began with Father Serra rising at dawn. He held a church service for the travelers while the cooks prepared breakfast. Then the soldiers and Indians saddled the horses and loaded supplies onto the backs of the mules.

Portola led the expedition riding on horseback at the front with Francisco Ortega, sergeant of the soldiers. Twenty soldiers followed in two rows. They were called *leatherjackets* for the buckskin jackets they wore. They carried shields and muskets and wore helmets.

The cook and his helpers rode behind the soldiers followed by a pack train of over one hundred mules. Food and supplies were lashed to their saddles. Muleteers and Indians kept watch over them.

A herd of horses came next followed by cattle. The Indian cowboys kept rounding up strays along the way. At the end, a dozen *leatherjackets* rode in the dust, guarding the people.

The expedition traveled slowly. The animals needed time to rest and graze. After lunch, the men unsaddled the horses and unloaded the mules. After eating, the men camped for the night.

Father Serra's leg became infected from an untreated insect bite. It pained him so much and weakened his health that Portola threatened to call off the expedition and return to Mexico. Father Serra pleaded with Portola and convinced a muleteer to treat his wound with medicine used for his mules. The leg improved and the expedition was able to continue. This injury troubled him for the rest of his life.

After traveling for forty-six days, the group arrived in San Diego on July 1, 1769. In the distance they could see the sails of two ships.

CALIFORNIA INDIAN TRIBES

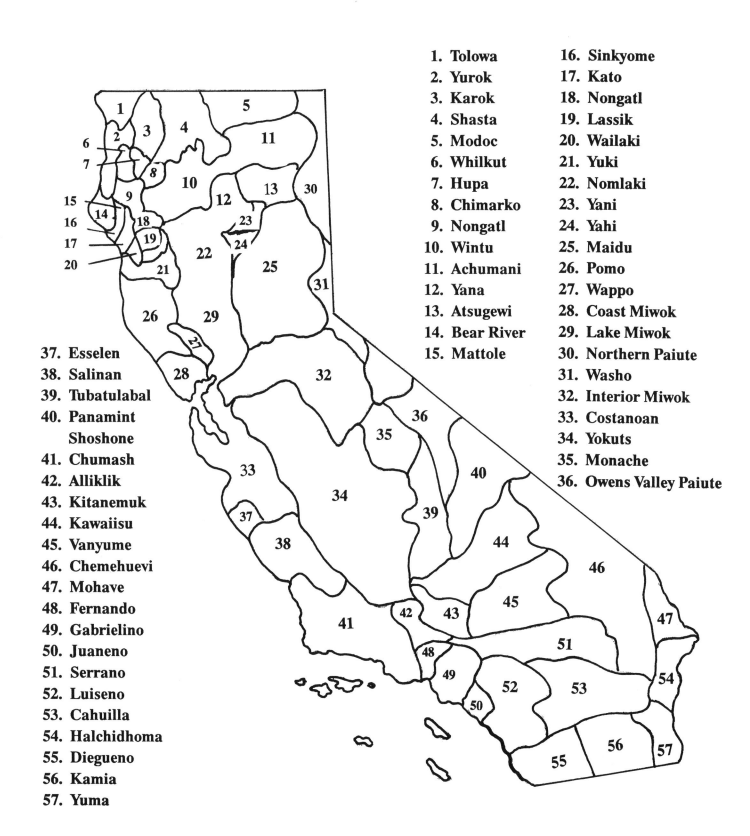

1. Tolowa	16. Sinkyome
2. Yurok	17. Kato
3. Karok	18. Nongatl
4. Shasta	19. Lassik
5. Modoc	20. Wailaki
6. Whilkut	21. Yuki
7. Hupa	22. Nomlaki
8. Chimarko	23. Yani
9. Nongatl	24. Yahi
10. Wintu	25. Maidu
11. Achumani	26. Pomo
12. Yana	27. Wappo
13. Atsugewi	28. Coast Miwok
14. Bear River	29. Lake Miwok
15. Mattole	30. Northern Paiute
	31. Washo
	32. Interior Miwok
	33. Costanoan
	34. Yokuts
	35. Monache
	36. Owens Valley Paiute

37. Esselen
38. Salinan
39. Tubatulabal
40. Panamint
    Shoshone
41. Chumash
42. Alliklik
43. Kitanemuk
44. Kawaiisu
45. Vanyume
46. Chemehuevi
47. Mohave
48. Fernando
49. Gabrielino
50. Juaneno
51. Serrano
52. Luiseno
53. Cahuilla
54. Halchidhoma
55. Diegueno
56. Kamia
57. Yuma

CHAPTER 3

INDIANS WERE LIVING ON THE LAND

When the Spaniards arrived, Indians were living on the land. How many Indians lived in California? It is believed that over 300,000 Indians lived in California when the Spanish missionaries first settled here in 1769. The Indians belonged to over fifty tribes. They spoke many different languages. A tribe is a group of people that speak the same language and have the same customs, territory, and name. Tribes in California numbered fewer people than many other states. We call them *tribelets* or small tribes. One hundred to one thousand people made up a *tribelet*.

Most Indian tribes welcomed the Spaniards. These gentle, independent people had never seen a white man before. They asked many questions. Who were they? What did they want? Why were they on Indian land? Their clothing and appearance must have looked strange to the California Indians.

The Spaniards whispered among themselves as they saw the Indians on the hillside. Carefully, the Indians wandered closer. First came the men who wore little or no clothing. The women followed closely behind dressed in deerskin skirts. Colorful paint and tattoos (marks on their skin) decorated their bodies.

Quickly, the Spaniards reached for the brightly-colored beads they had brought with them. They offered them as gifts to the Indians as a sign of friendship. The excited Indians picked up the sparkling beads and fingered them in the sunlight. They took them and ran off. Later they returned with food for the tired, hungry strangers.

brush house

bark house

plank house

LIFE IN AN INDIAN VILLAGE

California Indians lived together in villages similar to small towns. Indians of the same tribe would live in several villages. Usually 80-100 people lived in a village. The chief lived in the main village. The people of a village built houses, shared beliefs and customs, hunted, fished, gathered food, played, and worked. They obeyed the rules of the community.

The men's duties included hunting, fishing, and helping with major trips to gather acorns. They made weapons and tools for the family.

Women gathered plant foods, prepared and cooked food, wove baskets, made clothing, and raised the children. Families taught their children important lessons about how to survive off the land. They told them about the beliefs, customs, and stories of their tribe.

California Indians usually lived peacefully with their neighbors. They roamed freely within the land of their own tribe. Occasional fights with other tribes involved land rights, stealing, or unfair trading.

Houses

Some Indians lived simply in houses made of brush or tule grass. Other tribes built houses of plank or bark. What kind of house would they choose to build? This depended on their climate and what building materials were growing on their land. Indians living in warmer climates built brush houses. Those in colder weather built plank or bark houses to keep themselves warm. Several families usually lived together in one house.

Most villages built at least one sweathouse or *temescal*. Only men were allowed to use it except on ceremonial occasions. Inside, the men built a big fire in the center. The heat from the room caused them to sweat. Then they would run outside and jump into the cold water of a nearby ocean or lake. After this, they slept. The Indians thought it kept them clean and healthy.

A meeting house was built in every village. It was built large enough to hold everyone in the village. They gathered here for meetings, to tell stories, and perform dances or ceremonies.

Their food-gathering and hunting trips often took them away from their village. They built temporary houses for these trips. The Indians enjoyed living and working outdoors in good weather.

17

Hunting and Fishing for Food

The Indians spent much of their time looking for food since they did not plant crops. The men hunted with bows and arrows and trapped wild game. They trapped deer, rabbit, bear, mice, and birds. They used the skins and feathers of the animals for clothing and the bones for tools. Those living near the ocean, rivers, or lakes caught fish. They made tule, dug-out, and plank boats to help them fish. Their meals included more unusual food like grasshoppers, lizards, snakes, and worms.

Gathering Plant Food

While the men hunted and fished, the women gathered food. Many varieties of oak trees grew all over California. Most Indian tribes used the acorns from these trees as a main source of food. They gathered seeds and picked berries from the bushes. They pounded seeds, nuts, and acorns into meal. They prepared and cooked the meals.

The Indians took what the land had to offer them. Little went to waste. At times they did not have enough to eat. Their way of life could be hard. Then the Spaniards came. They offered food, shelter, and religion to any Indians who wanted to change their religion to Christianity. Many chose this life.

Arts and Crafts

Down by the river, the women choose reeds and brush. They used these materials to weave their baskets. Only women were allowed to make baskets. Like all California Indians, they wove beautiful baskets with difficult designs.

They wove them in all sizes and shapes for their many uses. Most were made in the shape of a bowl. They were made in colors of yellow, brown, black, and white. Only black needed to be dyed. They made it from a berry called elderberry. They used baskets to carry babies, hold food and water. They even wore them for caps. Since they did not have metal bowls, they used them for cooking.

Clay pots were seldom used among California Indians. They were used mainly to keep things in. They used a basket as a form to shape the clay. When the wet clay was dry, they put it in the fire to bake. Women taught their daughters and passed down the art of basketmaking. California Indians are considered to be among the most skilled basketmakers in the United States.

By custom, only men were allowed to carve bone and stone objects. Practically all tribes were found to do this. Southern tribes are especially known to have fashioned rock carvings and rock paintings in caves. It is thought to have been for religious and ceremonial reasons.

20

Games and Recreation

What kinds of games did California Indians like? They played ball games, guessing games, dice games, and gambled. Children swam in the ocean and rivers and played tag. They spun tops made from acorns and played a string game called cat's cradle.

Boys and men especially liked a game called *shinny*. It was sort of like field hockey. They marked off a playing area with posts on either end. Players (2-15) on two teams hit a wooden ball with curved sticks. The team who reached the post first with the fewest strokes won the game.

Hoop and pole was played with two players. Players took turns throwing a pole through a moving hoop made out of a willow branch. Each time the pole shot through the hoop, the player scored points.

Women favored dice games using pieces of shell, rocks, or hollowed-out nuts filled with tar. They painted dots on one side. The dice were shaken and tossed into a basket. Depending on how they landed, points were scored.

Ring and pin was a popular game played by women and children. A string was run through rings made of acorns or shells. It was attached to a pointed stick. The player would toss the rings up and try to catch them on the stick. These were just some of the many games Indians liked to play.

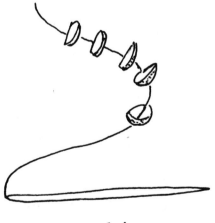

ring and pin game

21

Beliefs, Customs, and Ceremonies

Most California Indians believed in many gods. The gods lived as good and bad spirits in animals, plants, and nature. When a person became sick, the bad spirits took over their body. The village *shaman* or medicine man or woman was called upon. The Indians believed these people held special powers to heal the sick and talk to the gods. By using plant medicine, chanting, and dancing, the *shaman* would drive the evil spirits away.

California Indians did not have a written language or alphabet. They told their children about tribal customs and beliefs. Storytellers spun stories about how the world was created and the spirit world. Children listened closely to entertaining stories about coyote, eagle, and other animals.

Music held an important place in their lives. Indians made flutes, clappers, whistles, and drums. They played these instruments, sang or chanted songs, and danced for special days and for fun. Each tribe developed their own songs, chants, and dances.

On special days and important events, they celebrated with ceremonies like we celebrate holidays. Weddings, births, deaths, coming of age for boys and girls, hunting trips, harvest festivals, and war held special meaning for the Indians.

Not all California Indians came into contact with the Spaniards. Those living further in from the coast had little contact. It is thought that about 100,000 of the 300,000 Indians living in California became Christians during mission days. Many liked their old ways and chose to stay in their villages. If they decided to become Christians, the Indians had to move to a mission.

Not everyone who came to live at a mission liked it. Their new life was so different from the old. Sometimes the hard work seemed endless. The padres were always telling them what to do. For these reasons, some of the Indians changed their minds. They wanted to leave the mission.

The padres would not let them. They believed once the Indians decided to become Christians, they could not change their minds. Many Indians ran away. The soldiers galloped after them on horseback. They brought the runaways back and punished them. The Indians could not understand why they were treated so harshly. Other Indians liked the mission and wanted to stay.

CHAPTER 4

LIFE AT THE MISSIONS

The Indians who chose Christianity and came to live at a mission found many changes in their lives. The Indians had to work hard to keep the mission community going. For the first time they cleared the fields and planted crops. They learned crafts and trades in the workshops. They built buildings out of adobe bricks and cared for livestock. The Indians ate the food they raised, wove the clothes they wore, and lived in the houses they built. Their whole way of life was changed from what they had known in their villages.

At the beginning, each mission was given the supplies it needed to start. Two padres usually served at each mission. One taught the Indians Christianity. The other showed them how to do the work. From that time on, everything depended on their success! They supported themselves.

23

BUILDING THE MISSION

Temporary Shelters

Pounding, clanking, and chopping noises rang out as building began. Sweat dripped from the faces of the padres, soldiers, and Indians as they worked in the hot sun. The Indians came to help the white man build their buildings.

They started building shelters right away. The first buildings were built of wood, earth, and brush. Pine or other strong wooden posts were placed together then given a coating of clay earth. Bunches of tules or brush were attached to the top to form the roof. These shelters were used until the padres could build more lasting buildings of adobe bricks.

The Mission Plan

The Indians knew how to build simple grass huts. The padres wanted to build larger buildings out of adobe bricks for the mission. The Indians had never built houses like this before. Neither had the padres. The padres had to read books about building and design. From these they learned what to do. They drew up plans on paper to show the Indians.

The padre pointed to the drawing as he talked to the men. The church would go here, he explained. The padres' rooms, storehouses, housing for unmarried women, housing for boys, soldiers' barracks or rooms, and indoor workshops would all be built around a square called a quadrangle. He pointed to a place outside the square as the Indians gathered around him. If they chose to live at the mission, the married Indians would build their huts or adobe houses here.

The men looked to the land for materials to use for building the mission. Wood, stone, water, earth, and lime would be needed. In the forests grew trees for wood. The land provided them with clay earth and water to make their adobe bricks. Lime could be found in sea shells and a special kind of rock.

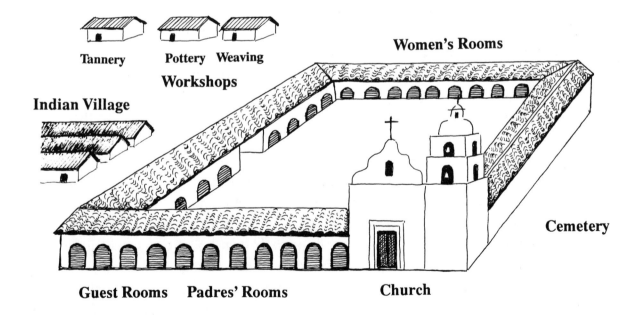

Tannery   **Pottery** **Weaving**   **Women's Rooms**

Workshops

Indian Village

Cemetery

Guest Rooms   **Padres' Rooms**   **Church**

25

Making Adobe Bricks

First, they needed to make adobe bricks. The padres, soldiers, and Indians stomped and pounded the clay earth with their hands and feet. They added water and straw. They mixed it together and poured it into a wooden mold. Out came an adobe brick 23 inches long, 11 inches wide, and 2-5 inches thick. The bricks were laid out in the sun to dry. Children sometimes helped scare off animals while the adobe bricks dried.

Other Indians gathered wood and built a blazing fire in the brick oven called a *kiln*. All day long they slid bricks in and out of the oven to bake. These bricks dried harder. They lasted longer than the sun-dried adobes. But they took more trouble to make.

The Indians clapped one adobe brick on top of another, slapping mud in between. They built the walls high and thick. Then they finished them with plaster. The plaster was made from a lime, water, and sand mixture. The lime was found in sea shells or a special kind of rock. On top of the walls, they piled straw for roofs. This is what they used for their own huts. But straw easily caught fire and burned up. Too many buildings burned along with them.

Later, tile roofs were used. They did not burn. The Indian women helped to get the clay earth ready. They mixed it with water. The men patted the wet clay on logs to shape them. They baked the wet tiles in the outdoor ovens until they were dry and hard.

Wood From The Forests

The Indian man hit the shining axe blade against the tree. It sliced the bark. Blow by blow the crack widened and gave way. The tree crashed to the ground. The men took the saw and cut the wood into long planks.

Pine and redwood were the most commonly used wood because of their strength and good supply. Some missions were located near large forests. Other missions had to haul lumber in from quite a distance. This was not an easy job when their only way to haul it was using a simple cart. These *carrietas*, were made of wood and used for carrying heavy objects. The oxen pulled the heavy load back to the mission.

The Spaniards brought tools with them like axes, iron wedges, saws, adzes, and other metal tools. The Indians had never seen tools like this before. They used stone and bone tools. The Spaniards showed the Indians how to use the metal tools to cut and shape beams, doors, and supports for roofs.

DAILY LIFE OF THE INDIANS

The ringing of the bells told the Indians it was time to wake up. The mission community began to come to life. Indian boys and girls, women, and men crowded into the church. The men and boys took their places together. Women and girls sat on the other side. Then all was quiet.

The church service began. The padre came out dressed in white satin robes sewn with red and gold flowers. These clothes were different from the dull gray robes he usually wore. Church was an important event. The padre chanted. Soon music and singing filled the air. The Indians said their prayers.

After church, everyone sat down at long wooden tables. Women from the kitchen dished out steaming hot corn mush into wooden bowls. They ate their fill. Afterward, the padres told them what work to do for the day.

Families headed different ways. The younger children ran off to learn Spanish and religious lessons from the padres. Adults began their work tasks.

At noon they all came together for lunch. The smell of hot *pozole* (stew) filled the air. The Indians sat at the table and spooned the tasty vegetables and beef down. After lunch everyone took a rest, a *siesta*. Then they went back to work for a few more hours.

In the late afternoon the Indians visited with friends and played games. They sat down to a dinner of corn mush and bread. At the end of the day, the bells rang calling the Indians to church.

28

WORK IN THE FIELDS

The hot sun shone down on the men in the fields as they hoed long rows of crops. A man guided the wooden plow as it dug into the rich, brown earth. An Indian in charge of the workers showed the other men how to do the work. He watched as they followed behind the plow. They dropped seeds of corn, wheat, beans, peas, and barley into holes. They covered them up with earth. The men watered, cared for, and picked the crops for the people to eat.

A good water system was important to the mission community. The land for the mission was partly chosen with a river nearby. People, animals, fields, orchards, and gardens all depended upon water. How did they get the water to the mission? At first the water system was simple. The Indians dug ditches and built damns. Later they built them with stone, adobe bricks, and clay pipes. Water flowed through them from the river into reservoirs (storage) at the mission or *lavenderias* (basins) where women washed clothes.

Nearby in the mission gardens Indians planted vegetables. Peas, tomatoes, beans, onions, melons, sweet corn, garlic, and red peppers grew in the gardens. The padres liked the Indians to keep family gardens too. Indians planted lemon, peach, orange, olive, fig, apple, plum, walnut, and almond trees.

Grapevines grew too. How did they make the grapes into wine? After picking them, the Indians put them in vats. They crushed the grapes with their feet. The juice escaped through an opening at the bottom into a barrel or oxhide. It was stored in barrels in dark cellars until it turned into wine.

Ripe olives were picked and dumped in the gristmill. They were crushed the same way as the wheat. Then they were put in sacks and placed in the olive press and squeezed. The oil that came out was used in cooking, for oil-burning lamps, and for oiling machines.

RAISING LIVESTOCK

Many Indians roamed the large mission lands carrying for cattle, sheep, oxen, and horses. Shephards walked on foot to care for the sheep. They tried to protect them from wild animals. They led them to places where they could eat grass and drink fresh water. During the spring, their heavy wool coats were cut off and made into blankets and clothing for the people at the missions.

Oxen, mules, and burros were used as work animals. Horses, however, were kept for riding and rarely used for heavy work. Chickens, pigs, and goats were kept nearby at the mission for food.

Cattle-raising became one of the most important industries at most of the missions. At first the livestock were kept near the mission corraled by low adobe walls. Later as the herds grew, animals were kept further out. That way, the animals could not nibble on crops growing in the fields.

Indian cowboys called *vaqueros* were taught to ride horses, rope, and herd the cattle. Often adobe houses for the cowboys, shepards, and their families were built away from the mission. It was easier for them to watch the animals and not have to travel back to the mission everyday.

Mexican settlers living on ranches near mission lands also raised cattle and livestock. Cattle strayed and ranch cattle mixed with mission cattle. Who did the cattle belong to? Each mission and ranch created its own brand. This special mark was burned into the tough hide of each animal with a branding iron. It showed who owned the animal. The animals were rounded up and branded several times a year. These occasions were called *rodeos*. After the branding, a great celebration took place.

30

PREPARING FOOD

What an enormous task to prepare food for the entire mission community! Several hundred to two thousand people needed to be fed three times a day! This task fell to the Indian women working in the kitchen.

The cattle, sheep, pigs, and chickens that the Indians raised fed the many people at the mission. Cattle were slaughtered for their beef. Fresh meat was barbecued over open grills. Meat that was not used was cut into strips, dipped in salty water, and left to dry. Jerky could be used when fresh meat was scarce.

Indians still hunted wild game such as deer, duck, and rabbit in much the same way as before mission times. They gathered wild fruits and nuts.

Vegetables, wheat, and fruit grown in the fields and orchards supplied the mission with food. Fruit was eaten fresh or dried. Grapes were made into raisins or wine. Olives pressed into oil were used in salads and for cooking oil.

At first, Indian women ground acorns like before mission days. Later they ground wheat and corn into flour. For this they used a *metate* and *mano*. A *metate* is a stone or volcanic slab on which corn or wheat is placed to grind. The woman takes a longer *mano* to mash the meal into a flour-like powder. They used knives, boards, spoons, and other wooden instruments.

Wheat was kneaded into flour for bread. The corn was mixed with water and made into a thin cake called a *tortilla*. *Torillas* were more commonly eaten than bread. A meal of *atole* and *tortillas* was often prepared. Chilies were added to flavor and spice up meals. Chocolate and honey sweetened foods.

Ovens built of bricks in a bee-hive shape had thick walls to hold the heat. The ovens could be found inside and outdoors at a mission.

WORK IN THE WORKSHOPS

Workshops burst with noise and activity. Indians worked in the blacksmith, carpentry, leather, pottery, tile, candle, and soap shops. They worked in the weaving rooms and in the tanning works.

Indian men were trained to be blacksmiths, carpenters, tanners, leather crafters, and builders. Women were trained to spin, weave, and sew. They worked hard at their trades and crafts. Without this work, the missions could not have been successful. Some missions specialized in certain trades like candlemaking and traded them with other missions for needed goods.

Blacksmith Shop

The blacksmith used iron and copper metals from Mexico to work with. He formed tools to be used in the workshops, fields, and for building. He fashioned hammers, nails, bolts, hinges, locks, keys, saws, picks, plowshares, and hoes. He also made kitchen tools.

Other useful objects for the mission included branding irons, pitchforks, knives, wrenches, and window gratings. He formed bits, stirrups, and horse-hoes for horses.

Preparing Cattle Hides

Raising cattle became the most important industry at many of the missions. The cattle were used for food, their hides for leather, and their fat to make candles and soap. Foreign ships visiting the coast of California traded goods for them.

How did the Indians prepare hides? They scraped the meat from the hides and soaked them in a salty liquid. Then they drove stakes into the ground to stretch the hides out to dry. Hides dried stiff. This was called *curing* the hides. Some hides were traded to the ships, while others were stored until they could be made into leather.

Tanning turns it into leather. How did the Indians do this? First, they soaked the hides in water to remove the salt used for curing them. Then they were placed in a lime liquid. After three or four days, the hides were removed and the loosened hair scraped off. The hides were washed and put in deep *vats* or pits lined with bricks in the ground.

Crushed oak bark was placed between each hide. Water was poured over them. The hides were left in the vats for 3-6 months. During this time, the water and oak bark were changed a few times. Finally, the hides were taken out and washed again and again. This time they were rubbed with tallow or oil. Now they were ready to be made into useful objects in the leather shop.

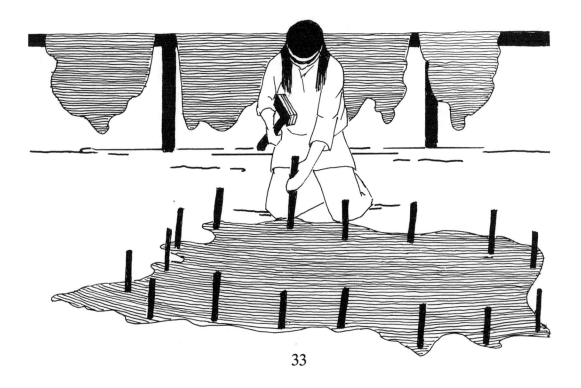

33

Leather Shop

In the leather shop men cut, hammered, and sewed leather into many useful objects. They made it into shoes, sandals, and sacks. Leather was also fashioned into saddles, harnesses, *reatas* or ropes used by the Indian cowboys.

Tallow

Fat from the cattle, sheep, hogs, and other animals was melted down into tallow. These fats were used for soapmaking and candlemaking. Indian women, men, and children gathered wood and built fires that had to be kept continually burning. Tallow became solid when it cooled. It was wrapped in hide bags and stored until it was needed for soap or candlemaking. Often it was traded with foreign ships.

Candlemaking

The small windows of the mission rooms let little light inside. Many candles were needed to light dark rooms and the church.

How were the candles made? An Indian heated the tallow or animal fat in a large metal kettle to melt it. The kettles were usually obtained in trade from whaling ships. Then he tied pieces of string to a wheel hanging above it. The candlemaker poured melted tallow on each string.

He turned the wheel and poured it on the next one. He let the tallow cool and poured on more. Little by little, the candles kept growing bigger. He stopped when he had the size he wanted.

Candlemaking was usually done during the cold months but not the rainy season. The fires needed to be kept burning all the time. Molds were sometimes used too.

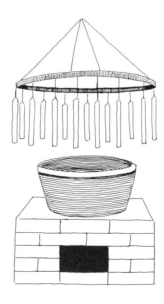

Soapmaking

Soapmaking, like candlemaking, was work saved for the cold months of the year. Solid tallow was usually taken from storage and placed in metal kettles, along with wood ashes from fires.

Fires were built under it and kept burning. Indian men, women, and children needed to gather much wood during the soapmaking.

The liquid was melted down. Then when it cooled, the soap floated on top of the water. The Indians skimmed it off then poured it into a mold. After it hardened, it was cut into bars. The bars of soap were stored on shelves until ready to use.

Weaving

Sheep were raised for food and clothing. In the springtime, the wool coats of the sheep were sheared. Many people were needed to cut the wool off the sheep and prepare it. The men did the shearing with handmade steel shears brought from Mexico.

The women and female children usually took over the preparation of the wool. After the wool was removed from the sheep, the wool was loaded into the carreta and taken to the mission.

Children helped pick off the thorns and sticks in the wool. Then it was placed in large kettles with soap and water to be washed. Afterwards, it was hung out to dry on drying racks or on top of the bushes. When dry, the wool was straightened or carded before spinning into yarn.

The click-clack of the wooden loom could be heard as an Indian woman moved it back and forth. Looms were built by Spanish carpenters. Mostly women wove rough blue wool into cloth. They talked among themselves as they combed, carded, and spun the wool into yarn. Some women dyed the yarn. The dyes to color the material were produced from plants and flowers growing nearby.

Others cut the cloth and sewed it into clothes. Women made also made gray robes for the padres. Skillful weavers wove blankets in bright colors. At some missions, the Indians also wove cotton material too.

37

Carpentry Shop

Wooden doors and beams for building and repairing the mission were sawed and shaped here. Chairs, tables, and other rough furniture were made in the carpentry shop too. Often furniture and other goods were obtained from trading ships sailing along the coast of California. These ships came from England, Spain, and other countries. They wanted to trade their goods for the hides and tallow produced at the missions.

Pottery Shop

The pottery shop was important to the building and repair of mission buildings and water channels. Indians used molds to make both roof and floor tiles. They made clay pipes for the water to flow through for use in the water channels. The Indians fit them together and sealed them with pitch.

Kilns were kept here to fire the adobe bricks. The Indians had little time left over to make pottery jars, though some were made here for use in the kitchen.

GAMES AND RECREATION

In the late afternoon work was finished. Men, women, and children gathered in the courtyard to visit and play games. What kinds of games did mission Indians play? They played most of the same games they had played before mission times. They still played tag, ran foot races, and swam in the ocean. Even though the padres didn't like it, the Indians still gambled. They played dice games, guessing games, shinny, hoop and pole, and many other games.

Both adults and children joined in games of tug-of-war. Boys and men on one side challenged girls and women on the other side of the rope. They pulled the rope back and forth until one side toppled over.

They still danced and sang in celebrations. Now the Indians liked the Spanish *fiestas* or parties. On church holidays the mission rang with laughter and excited shouts. The Indians played games. Spanish bear and bullfights were staged. At night the square glowed with candles for dancing. Work was forgotten and left for another day.

THE SOUNDS OF MUSIC

The sound of flutes filled the air. Indians carved flutes out of animal bone and wood. It is not surprising that California Indians enjoyed music at the mission. They loved the songs, hymns, and chants the padres taught them. They sang at work, in church, and for fun. It had always been an important part of their daily lives.

Here at the mission, it was still an important part of their lives. At the mission the Indians sang and played in the church choir. What a great many instruments to choose from! They plucked the strings of violins and harps, violas, and basses. They clanged and played cymbals, triangles, and drums.

The padres helped them make violins since there were few of these. They longed to play the barrel organ with its strange sounds.

The bells rang all day long. The Indians could tell by the bells when to go to church, to eat, and to work. Bells were rung for visitors, on special days, and important events. Bells came in all sizes, shapes, and sounds. Some bells were large and heavy. The bell ringer who rang these had to move quickly away to miss getting hit. The Indians thought it an honor to be chosen to ring the bells.

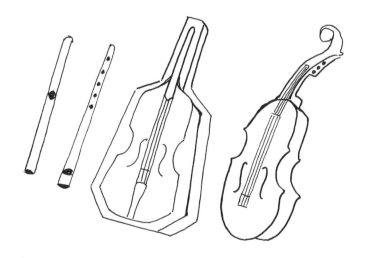

carved bone flute, five-stop flute, bass viol, violin

41

THE ART OF THE INDIANS

An Indian dipped his brush into the red paint and carefully stroked it on the church wall. Then he leaned back to look at his artwork. He added blue paint. He had mixed the paints from the flowers and plants he gathered. He squeezed the juice from a flower into the pot. Then he mixed it with olive oil. The bright designs colored the plain adobe walls.

Artists carved wood and stone statues. They made beautiful objects for the church and missions.

Women still wove baskets as they had in pre-mission times. Everyone worked hard for the mission community. On special days they visited their old villages. Some of the Indians wished they could live there with their old friends. The padres would not allow it.

THE MISSIONS

Each mission has its own story to tell. The story of the missions is really the story of the people. It is about the Indians and the padres who lived, struggled, and even died out in the wild lands of early California.

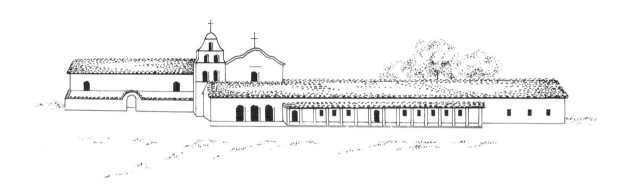

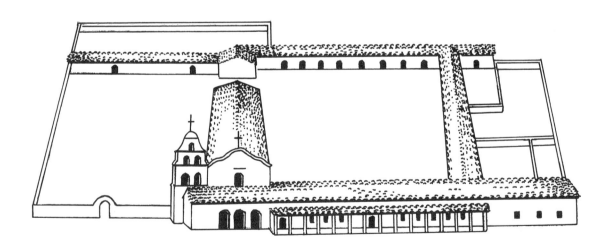

Mission San Diego de Alcala during mission days

CHAPTER 5

SAN DIEGO DE ALCALA

First Mission, founded July 16, 1769

Portola's land expedition with Father Serra arrived in San Diego. The men felt tired, sick, and hungry from their rough journey. They shouted with joy when they saw the ships, the *San Antonio* and the *San Carlos,* anchored in the bay. As they drew closer, they were saddened by what they found.

Many of the sailors lay sick or dying of a disease called scurvy. Stormy weather and old maps had made it difficult to find San Diego. This lengthened their voyages. The supply ship, the *San Jose,* was lost at sea.

Some of the men still needed rest and care. They stayed behind in San Diego. The excitement of adventure caused others to go on. Captain Portola gathered up some of the soldiers and set out in search of Monterey Bay. The ship, the *San Antonio*, was sent back to Mexico for more supplies to help the group survive.

Father Serra planted a cross in the ground and blessed it. The first mission had now been founded in the new land.

Diegueno Indians living nearby came to visit the mission. These visits were not friendly. The Indians did not like the Spaniards on their land. Neither the Indians nor the Spaniards could understand each other. They spoke different languages. The Indians wanted them to leave.

The expedition could not find Monterey Bay. The discouraged men came back to San Diego. They found many men were starving and others dead. The supply ship that was to bring food had never come. Portola insisted they must give up and go back to Mexico.

Father Serra pleaded with him. The Indians would never know Christianity if the missions were not founded. Finally, he talked Portola into waiting a few days. Surely the ship would come by then. It was the last day before they were to go back. The white sails of a ship suddenly came into sight. Shouting and cheering broke out among the men. The ship, the *San Antonio*, had come in time.

The ship brought food, medicine, and supplies. Captain Portola and his men started out again for Monterey. Father Serra wanted to go with them this time.

They left two padres and a group of soldiers behind to run the new mission. They planted seeds for crops to feed the people. The crops did not grow well. The land had too little water and poor soil. Trouble with the soldiers at the *presidio* developed. For these reasons, the padres decided to move the mission and build a new one a few miles away.

Not many Indians came. As time passed, the Indians became less friendly. Their leaders did not like the padres telling their people what to do. They did not want them to give up their old religion.

On the night of November 5, 1775, an angry band of Indians attacked the mission. Fire blazed! Arrows and gunfire flew through the air.

Padre Luis Jayme rushed out to try to stop the Indians. "Love God, my children!" he shouted before he died.

The bows and arrows of the Indians could not match the strength of the Spaniards' guns. Many people were killed. Wounded from both sides lay bleeding. The Indians lost, but they brought those who were hurt to the mission for help. The Indians were friendlier to the white man after the battle. Still, not many wanted to live at the mission.

The wheat swayed back and forth in the afternoon wind. Yellow cornstalks shot up to the blue sky. The new land was good for farming. Olive trees produced some of the best olive oil. Cattle grew fat on the green grass. The mission could now supply food and products for the people. Trades were never good at this mission.

What about the Indians? Would they always be unfriendly? Would they never know Christianity? Father Serra hoped not.

A young Indian boy visited often at the mission. Father Serra taught him Spanish. He asked the boy to find an Indian couple who would be interested in having their child baptized.

Father Serra happily waited for the event. The baptism ceremony is given for a person to become a Christian. Father Serra dipped his hand in the baptismal bowl to sprinkle holy water on the baby's head. Suddenly, an Indian ran up and snatched the baby away from Father Serra. The Indian ran off with it. The baby was never baptized. This event saddened the padre.

During the year 1797 the padre recorded a time of growth. Five hundred and sixty-five new Indians came to live at the mission. That brought the total population of Indians to 1,400 people. Crops grew well and livestock increased to 20,000 sheep, 10,000 cattle, and 1,250 horses.

This mission grew slower than most and was not as successful. By 1827 it started to decline. When Mexico became independent from Spain, the padres were told to leave the mission. For years weeds grew on the land. Walls of mission buildings crumbled and fell. The government gave the mission away to Santiago Arguello. They gave it to him for his good service to the government. When the U.S. took over California, the military occupied it from 1846-1862.

47

TODAY AT THE MISSION

Singing fills the old adobe church once more during church services. The church is small and plain inside. The beams and altar are handpainted. The padres who served the mission are buried in the floor. This was a custom of early California.

Outside, the adobe building looks simple. The tall bell tower climbs to 46 feet high. Five bells hang inside. The largest one weighs over 1,000 pounds.

A small museum displays vestments or church clothes of the padres, Indian pottery and baskets, and religious objects.

The mission sits up on a hill. To the right of the entrance is a garden with a white cross to honor Father Jayme, the padre killed during an Indian attack.

A walk in the garden out back will find a statue of Father Serra. He was the first President of the Missions. The Indian graveyard nearby is the oldest one in California. A fountain is shaded by many pepper trees.

Remains of the adobe walls and tile floors of a building have been uncovered. These diggings or excavations are thought to have been the padres' living quarters, library, and guest rooms.

Part of the dam constructed in early days can be seen east of the mission. Be sure to visit the Serra Museum located nearby, a museum about Father Serra. It stands on land believed to be the first location of the mission.

Cross honoring Father Jayme

Excavations or diggings to find old mission buildings

49

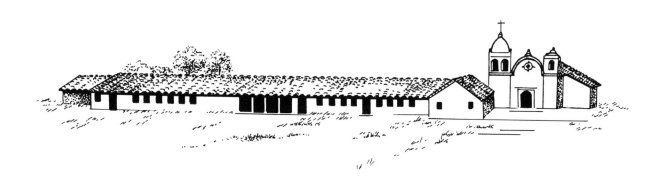

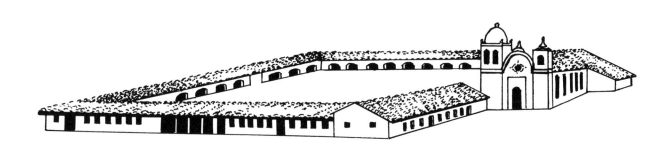

Mission   San Carlos Borromeo during mission days

CHAPTER 6

SAN CARLOS BORROMEO (CARMEL)

Second Mission, founded June 3, 1770

The tall, green pine trees could be seen in the distance. The water of the bay sparkled clear and blue. The men aboard the ship cheered! At last they had found Monterey Bay. They settled near its banks for a short time.

First, the men realized they must solve the problem of food. It took time to plant crops and for them to grow. Game ran wild on the new land. Why not go hunting? The men organized a hunting party. They headed for the Valley of the Bears. They returned leading mules loaded down with 6,000 pounds of bear meat for the mission.

The following year, they moved the mission to Carmel Valley. Here in the natural forest setting they did not have any of the troubles of the old land. There had been no water on the other land, and the soil was poor. On the new land a river flowed with fresh water. The rich soil brought them good crops.

Father Serra chose this mission as his home when he was not off founding other missions. He learned the language of the Eslenes Indians who lived near the mission. He wanted to tell them about Christianity. The Indians were friendly, and he hoped they would want to accept the new religion.

A stone craftsman from Mexico was sent for to design a new church. Manuel Ruiz hammered and carved the yellow stone, showing the Indians how to build the church. The stone, sandstone, was quarried from the nearby Santa Lucia Mountains. The finished church looked grand! A window shaped in a star fit in the center. The rays of sunlight shone through it. The unusual style made it look different from any other mission church.

"Pirates! Pirates!" a messenger cried. Bouchard, the French pirate and his men attacked the Fort of Monterey in 1818. They burned buildings, killed people, and stole what they found. Would the pirates come to the mission close by?

The padres and Indians feared the pirates. Quickly, they hid the treasures of the church and left. When the danger was over, they returned to find the mission had not been touched.

When Father Fermin de Lasuen became President, he kept the plan of the mission system. He walked many miles to found nine other missions.

A year after the pirates came to Monterey, the mission began to decline. Indians began to leave. The mission as a self-sufficient community was failing.

After the Mexican government took over, the padre and the rest of the Indians left. The roof caved in and the buildings began to fall apart. Birds nested in the ruins, and squirrels scampered through holes in the walls.

TODAY AT THE MISSION

Mission San Carlos Borromeo will long be remembered in history. Many a tired, hungry traveler stopped here for the night. There were no hotels in those days. This is where the presidents of the missions usually lived.

During the 1930s, the major rebuilding of the mission took place under a man named Harry Downie. Today, there is much to see. The worn, leather-bound books in glass cases make up California's first library. Father Serra brought many of the books with him to the new country.

Reminders of him are everywhere. Inside the chapel a statue shows him dying. It is called a sarcophagus and is created in bronze and stone. His friends are gathered around him. The symbol of California, the grizzly bear, lies at his feet. A tiny bare room like the one he lived in can be seen at the mission. Outside in the garden is an excellent statue of him near the entrance.

Another room displays a mission kitchen. Baskets and tools the Indians used are also shown.

Beautiful gardens frame this mission by the sea. Many visitors think this is the most beautiful of all the missions. Most people call it the Carmel Mission because that is the town in which it can be found.

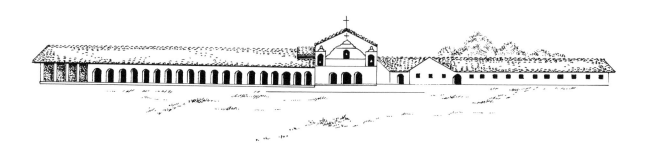

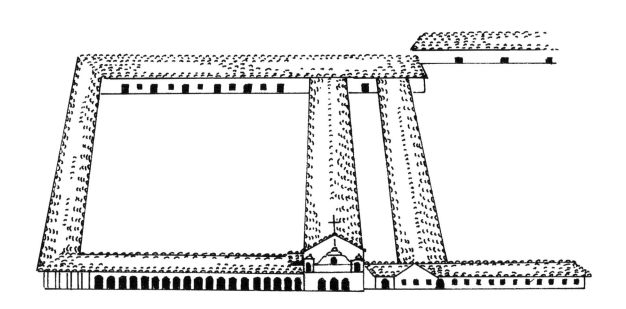

Mission San Antonio de Padua during mission days

CHAPTER 7

MISSION SAN ANTONIO DE PADUA

Third Mission, founded July 14, 1771

The Spaniards bent down to unpack their supplies. Two men lifted the bells and tied them to a tree. The mission land had been chosen. Father Serra walked to the tree and pulled the ropes to ring the bells. They clanged loudly. Enthusiastically, he shouted for the Indians to come. No one was in sight except the Spaniards.

Soon a young Indian boy who had heard the ringing of the bells walked toward them. After the ceremony, Father Serra gave the boy a gift of colored glass beads. He took them and went away. Later he returned with many other Indians. They offered the travelers pine-nuts, grains, and rabbits for food. From the beginning, the Indians living around this mission showed friendliness to the padres.

Father Serra went on his way, leaving in charge Fathers Miguel Pieras and Buenaventura Sitjar. Building started at once. Within several weeks the people had built a storehouse, chapel, and rooms for padres and soldiers. The Indians helped with the building.

A good beginning was spoiled by poor weather the first year. Either the hot sun burned down on them or the freezing cold chilled them. The water dried up and the crops failed.

The next year, they moved the mission near the San Miguel Creek. What a beautiful scene it made set among the mountains! Pine and oak trees grew on the land. The thump of axes hitting the trees echoed as the men chopped them down. They used wood and dry brush to build shelters until adobe buildings could be constructed.

Often the land chosen for the mission was not good enough. The soil would not grow crops. No stream or river flowed through the land for water. Many missions had to be moved for these reasons.

Each mission had to raise its own food and make goods in the workshops that it would need. The Spanish government would not give them money to run them.

This mission made fast and steady progress for the first five years. In time they built more living quarters, guest rooms, workshops, and storerooms.

The mission built a water channel to bring water closer to the fields for the crops. Water flowed down the hills through clay pipes carrying it from the San Antonio River to the mission. It stretched for three miles. The water-powered mill they built to grind the grain became one of the first of its kind in California.

One of the reasons for the success of the mission was Father Sitjar. He served the mission well for 37 years. Learning the Mutsun language spoken by the local Indians, he was able to teach them Christianity. He wrote down the words to their language forming the first dictionary in that language. He was an excellent leader and the Indians loved him.

The weather still sometimes troubled them. One Easter in 1780, the wheat crop was almost destroyed by a cold frost. They kept flooding the fields with water to thaw it out. Then they prayed for nine days in the church. Their crop that year was a better one than ever before. This helped give the Indians faith.

Beautiful Palomino horses galloped across the mission lands shaking their manes in the wind. The Indians took pride in feeding, grooming, and caring for their prized horses. They also raised large herds of cattle and sheep.

This mission grew to become one of the largest missions. The years from 1802-1805 proved the best. During those years, over one thousand Indians lived at the mission. The Mexican government took over the missions after Mexican Independence. The padres left. Indians all over California were given the right to vote but few were allowed to. San Antonio is the only mission known to have held an election that let the Indians vote.

TODAY AT THE MISSION

The mission looks like a small town today. It is one of the best restored of all the missions. The patio, quadrangle, and church are restored. The *convento* serves as a museum.

The clanging of a blacksmith's tools at work is missing. Visitors can see where he made useful metal objects like saws and axes in his shop. In the tile workshops clay tiles for roofs and water pipes took their shape. Tools used by the Indians stand as models today. A gristmill was used for crushing wheat and making it into flour. An olive press squeezed olives for making olive oil. Candles made from tallow hang over the kettle as they did in mission days. A spinning wheel and weaving loom can be seen. Indian women wove wool, flax, and cotton into clothes and blankets.

A padre's room and kitchen displays recreate other mission rooms. Minature model displays show how some of the Indians performed their daily activities at the mission. A gristmill, olive press, rip saw, well and water reservoir are among them.

The background of the mission is set against a high mountain peak. Junipero Serra Peak is named for the founder of the missions. Sailors in the early days used it as a point to steer their ships toward. They gave the mission gifts of carved wooden statues called figureheads from their ships to thank them for a safe journey.

San Antonio is the only mission located on a military reservation. It shares land with the Hunter Liggett Military Reservation. Out in the country, it is as peaceful and isolated as it was back in mission days. This is one of the most fascinating missions to visit in the chain. Located near the town of Jolon, it is one of the most expertly and fully restored.

rip saw

Candle display (top) and Mission San Antonio today (bottom)

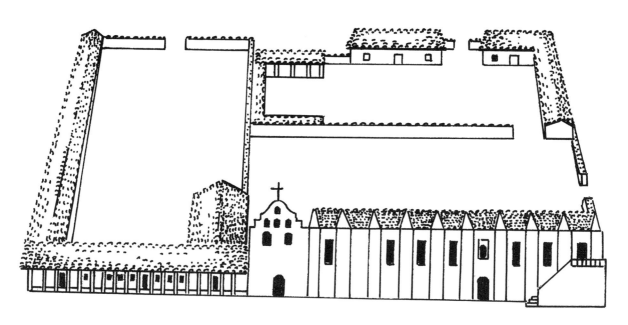

Mission San Gabriel Arcangel during mission days

60

CHAPTER 8

SAN GABRIEL ARCANGEL

Fourth Mission, founded September 8, 1771

The Spaniards came into view. Suddenly, a shower of arrows flew at them. The Indians were attacking! Quickly a padre pulled out the painting of Mary, Mother of Jesus. He held it up for the Indians to see.

What happened next seemed like a miracle. When the Indians saw the painting, they threw down their bows and arrows. They looked at it closely, admiring its beauty. They offered the strangers their friendship. Now the painting is over three hundred years old. It is hung inside the church to remember that day.

The *queen* of the missions during its good times became the richest of all the missions. It produced more crops than any other mission. Great cattle herds wandered on the lands. More wine was made here than at any other mission. Indians kept busy in the workshops. The soap and candlemaking workshops supplied many of the missions with their goods.

But there was trouble at this mission. One of their biggest problems was the soldiers. They were supposed to keep order, but they could not get along with the Indians. They bullied them and made fun of them. They punished them for little reason. The Indians did not like this.

Once a soldier hurt the wife of an Indian chief. This angered the chief. He gathered together a few members of his tribe and tried to attack the soldier. The soldiers fired their guns at the Indian, and the chief was killed.

61

This upset the Indians and Father Serra. It never should have happened. He complained to the governor in Mexico. The soldier was punished. But by then, the Indians did not trust the white man. For a long time, few Indians came to the mission.

Settlers traveled here from Mexico. They farmed and built towns called *pueblos* in California. Spain at this time owned Mexico and wanted more people to come to California. They needed a strong claim to the land.

Settlers lived near the mission in the nearby *pueblo* of Los Angeles. Most of them were good people. Others caused problems. They hired Indians so they would not have to do the hard work of farming their land. The Indians were not paid much for their work.

The more troublesome of the settlers always complained. They said the padres did not take care of their religious needs. They accused the padres of cutting off their water supply. Neither of the charges was true.

Governor Pio Pico claimed the land for Mexico. On May 4, 1846, he broke the law. He sold the mission to pay his debts. San Gabriel was the mission where he had been born and baptized.

TODAY AT THE MISSION

Visitors stop to feed the pigeons that flock in the courtyard and gardens. The church stands in the background. Heavy supports hold it up against the many earthquakes that have shaken its walls. Four earthquakes shook the land on the day it was founded. On October 1, 1987, another earthquake struck, the Whittier-Narrows Earthquake. It heavily damaged the mission. Repairs to the mission buildings are continuing.

A famous collection of paintings is owned by the mission. An unknown Christian Indian mixed paints and brushed them on the sails taken from a ship. Fourteen paintings tell the story of Jesus Christ. They are the oldest religious paintings created by a California Indian artist.

Outside, a cannon called a *frijolera* is one of the weapons that was used by the soldiers. It can still be seen on the grounds.

The outdoor kitchen is displayed with model kettles similar to those used for cooking in mission days. The remains of the tanning works can also be viewed.

At one time the mission lands grew to 90 acres. Times have changed. The nearby *pueblo* of Los Angeles grew into the large city of Los Angeles. Cities of San Gabriel, Alhambra, and Monterey Park stand on soil that once belonged to the mission. The mission is named for the angel, Gabriel. According to the Bible, the angel carried the news to Mary that she was to have a son named Jesus.

Display of kettles for outdoor cooking and boiling tallow

Mission San Luis Obispo de Tolosa during mission days

CHAPTER 9

SAN LUIS OBISPO

Fifth Mission, founded September 1, 1772

The generous Indians spread their wild nuts and grain on grass mats before the Spaniards to eat. The hungry white men reached for handfuls of food. They ate until their stomachs were filled.

The Indians remembered when the white man had first come to this valley. Fierce bears roamed the land and scared them. The bows and arrows of the Indians could not pierce the tough skins of the bears. The soldiers had come to hunt bear. They had killed many bears. They had taken the meat back to the hungry people of the Carmel and San Antonio Missions. The Indians were thankful and friendly to the Spaniards.

Explorers carefully chose land watered by two streams that flowed among the trees. The rich, brown soil would be good for growing crops. Many friendly Indians lived here including Chumash and other tribes. Maybe they would want to come to the mission.

In the beginning, the Indians did not come. Five soldiers and two Indians started to build. The mission did not have much to interest them. They were friendly but did not care about the new religion.

After the crops of corn and beans were planted at the mission, the Indians began to come. Food sometimes drew the Indians to the missions. The Indians had to find and gather their own food. Sometimes much game and food could be found in the wilds. At other times, the Indians went hungry.

Other Indians were not as friendly. Three times the mission was attacked by angry Indians. In 1776, 1778, and 1782 Indians shot fire arrows onto tule grass roofs. Many of the buildings, food, and tools burned up in these fires. Mission Indians helped to put the fires out.

The reason these Indians attacked the mission was they believed the white man was their enemy. He was trying to take their land. This was their way of showing the Spaniards they wanted them to go away. The Spaniards did not go away. They built more buildings. They made curved tiles for roofs instead of grass. These did not burn. All the missions used this kind of roof by 1784.

Father Cavaller served here alone for the first seventeen years. After he died, Father Luis Martinez came to the mission. The Indians gathered around him laughing and talking. Sometimes he joined in their games. His friendliness brought many Indians to the mission. He was a brave man too. Once he led a group of mission Indians to defend several missions against attack by pirates.

An Indian man ran into the courtyard shouting. The men of the Indian village gathered around to hear what he had to say. The man who spoke was an *alcalde*. By 1780 the Indians could elect these leaders called *alcaldes*. It was like we elect people today to represent us in government. During the day, *alcaldes* would visit the padres and learn the news and orders. At the end of the day, they would shout it out at the Indian villages. They also served as policemen to keep order among their people. Less important leaders called *regiodores* helped them.

This was a good way for the Indians to learn how to govern themselves. The padres at the beginning hoped the Indians would be able to run the missions alone in time.

At first, the padres taught the Indians trades. During the 1790s, Mexican artists and workers came to teach crafts and trades to the Indians. They taught them ironwork, leathermaking, tanning, weaving, carpentry, and building. The skills they taught the Indians were important in helping the missions support themselves.

The padre sat at his desk and dipped the point of his feather pen in the black ink. Carefully he wrote on the paper: wheat, 1300 bushels; corn, 300 bushels; and cattle, 700 head. He marked down the amounts of all the crops and livestock of the mission for that year.

He turned to the church records. How many people were born that year? How many were baptized, had married or died? The padre wrote it down. Then he closed the books. He was finished for the year. The government made a law that each year the padres had to write these reports. It helps us know today how well the mission progressed.

Indians at other missions became unhappy with their lives. The Chumash Indians at Santa Ines and La Purisima missions attacked their missions. The Indians at San Luis Obispo seemed happy. They did not want to join in the attack.

Their happiness soon ended. The Mexican government took the mission and arrested Father Martinez. They said things about him that were not true. They accused him of taking money and killing mission cattle. He was sent back to Spain. They wanted to get rid of him so he could no longer protect the Indians. Some of the settlers took their land. In 1845 Governor Pio Pico sold everything except the church for a total of $510.

TODAY AT THE MISSION

The chapel and some of the land was returned to the Catholic church after the American government took over. The mission church and part of the *convento* can be seen today. The mission sits in the middle of the Mission Plaza on Monterey and Chorro Streets in downtown San Luis Obispo.

A side wing to the L-shaped church has been added since mission days. Inside, there are many art treasures to see. The 14 Stations of the Cross are the original. Altar bells on a wheel, made of metal and wood, can be turned by a handle. Tall candle holders made of brass or wood and other religious objects date from mission days.

The statue of St. Louis Obispo, for whom the mission was named, stands behind the altar. Though born an Italian prince, he chose to become a priest.

The partially restored *convento,* where the padres used to sleep, is now a museum. A display of photographs of the mission show how it changed over the years. Indian baskets, arrowheads, and farm tools are shown. These are what the Indians used to do their work. Original window frames made of rawhide are displayed. They were stretched like paper over wooden frames.

Outside, olive trees sway in the wind. They are the first ones planted in California. Can you imagine the Indians picking them back in mission days? The mission was known for its fine olive groves, orchards, and vineyards.

The church is still used for services, and elementary and high schools stand on the mission land in the city of San Luis Obispo.

Mission San Luis Obispo today

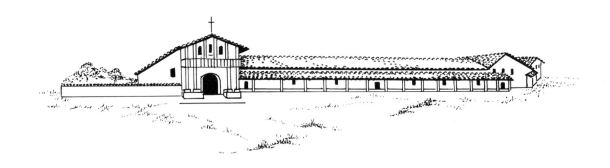

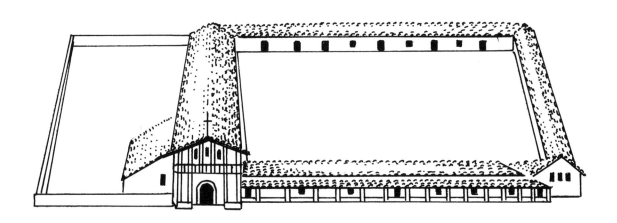

Mission San Francisco de Asis during mission days

CHAPTER 10

SAN FRANCISCO DE ASIS (DOLORES)

Sixth Mission, founded June 29, 1776.

A large expedition moved slowly toward San Francisco. The group of men, women, and children came along with the padres and soldiers on the trip. The hooves of the cattle pounded and stirred up dust as they plodded along the trail. The herd would be for the new mission.

The people pitched their tents near a river. Colonel Juan Bautista de Anza named the river, Arroyo de los Dolores. The name stuck, and Mission Dolores is still the name it is usually called. Colonel Anza brought over two hundred people with him from Mexico. He dropped some of the settlers off in Monterey then continued on to San Francisco. Soon sailing ships would come with more people and supplies. They would build a *presidio* or fort nearby.

Several different dates are given for the founding of the mission. The real founding date is uncertain. It is thought that the mission site was decided on June 29, 1776. The official order to found it was delayed by Captain Rivera, the military commander of California. Father Francisco Palou founded it anyway and held a ceremony on October 9, 1776.

No Indians came to the founding ceremony. Where had they gone? Enemy Indians had attacked and burned their village. Many of their people were killed. Others ran away. A month later the Indians returned. They came to visit the strangers many times. They took things from the new settlers. The soldiers fired their guns and hurt several Indians. For a while they feared the white people.

71

Mission Dolores never became a rich mission. Many troubles disturbed the mission. The cold, foggy weather and sickness bothered the Indians. The earth was sandy and poor for farming.

The Coastonoan Indians who lived here fished for much of their food. Waves crashed against their canoes. Quickly, they steered their boats through the foamy water. They dipped their baskets and nets into the sea to catch sardines. They made fishhooks from shells. With these they caught whitefish, sea-bream, and other kinds of fish. The Indians also carved spears of bone to catch fish.

They raised cattle to eat for food. The hides and tallow gave them products to trade to ships and other missions. Women skillfully tanned animal hides. They soaked them in lime water to loosen the hair. Then they scraped it off with a metal tool. The hide was stretched on the ground by pounding wooden stakes along the sides. It was left out in the sun to dry. Indians made soap and candles from the tallow too.

After Father Serra's death, Father Palou left this mission to return to Mexico. He wanted to write a book about his friend's life. Fathers Martin Landaeta and Antonio Dante came in 1785. During this time many buildings were completed. They treated the Indians stricter and not as kindly as Father Palou.

The Spaniards brought sickness to the mission. The Indians' shuddered from fever and chills of measles and smallpox. They lived closely together so sickness spread quickly. This frightened the Indians to see so many people dying. Many ran away. In ten years, only a few hundred Indians remained.

Something needed to be done! North of San Francisco the padres found land with good weather warmed by sunshine. It was quiet and peaceful in San Rafael. Buildings were built for another mission. This one functioned more like a hospital. Sick Indians came here to rest. Many Indians got well.

Should Mission Dolores be closed? This question was asked. With all its problems and bad weather, it might be best. The government and padres argued. Finally, they decided to keep it open.

After many of the Indians went to live at Mission San Rafael, Mission Dolores never recovered from the loss of Indians. Around 6,500 Indians were baptized here, 2,000 Indians married, and over 5,000 Indians buried during the mission years.

TODAY AT THE MISSION

Mission Dolores was a lonely spot in mission days. Few travelers came here. The California Gold Rush finally woke up this sleepy village. It turned it into the busy city of San Francisco.

The old mission church, a small museum, and graveyard are all that is left of mission days.   The church is unusual in design with mission, Moorish, and Corinthian styles of building used. Inside the mission church the Indian artwork is original, though it has been retouched with paint. The ceiling and beams are painted in colors of red, blue, white, and yellow. The hand-carved altar and its statues were brought from Mexico.

Outside in the graveyard stand many headstones and statues. A statue of Father Serra was created by a blind sculptor. One of an Indian woman represents the unmarked graves of 5,000 Indians who are buried here.

Next to the old church stands a new one. Many people worship here today. The two churches stand side by side. One tells of the past life, the other the present. This mission was named after St. Francis, who founded the Franciscan religious order of priests.

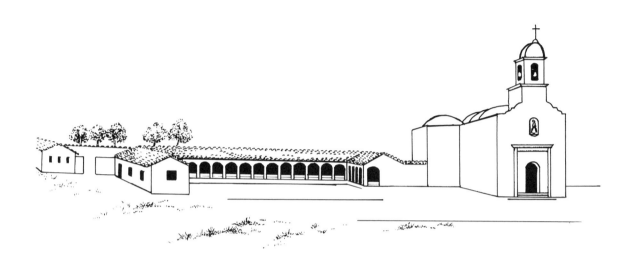

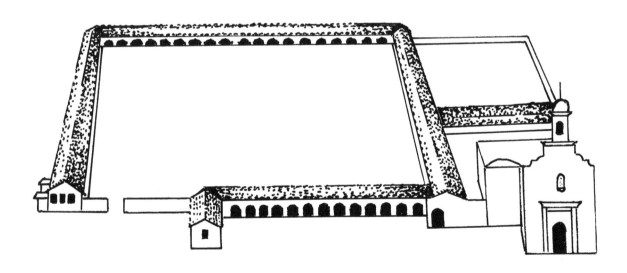

San Juan Capistrano Mission during mission days

74

CHAPTER 11

SAN JUAN CAPISTRANO

Seventh Mission, founded November 1, 1776

Eight days after the mission founding, a horseman galloped into their camp. "Indian attack, Indian attack!" he shouted. "Mission San Diego is on fire!"

The padres at San Juan Capistrano did not know if they would be attacked too. They quickly buried the mission bells and hurried to the fort at San Diego. The soldiers at the fort would protect them. The mission would have to wait to be founded.

A year later the padres returned. Many Indians came to the mission within a short time. This mission enjoyed success from the beginning. Acres of fruit trees were planted in long rows. Juicy red and green grapes grew on the vines. The rich crops fed the people well.

The mission community was a busy place to live. The Indians worked at their trades in the indoor and outdoor workshops. They spun, wove, sewed, and carved wood. They became good wagonmakers, blacksmiths, shoemakers, winemakers, and olive-oil makers.

Many herds of cattle roamed the grassy lands. Hides from cattle were stretched in the sun to dry. The Indians made them into leather goods such as saddles and sandals. Sometimes they traded the products to other missions.

Every part of the cattle was used. The fat and bones were boiled down into tallow in brick pits. They made soap and candles from it.

In the blacksmith's shop they made metal objects like locks, keys, and iron bars. The smelter was a brick pit used to heat the metal.

An olive crusher was used to make olive oil. First the Indians washed the olives and stuffed them into woolen bags. They put them in a press and turned it. Out came the olive oil. It was used for cooking in the mission kitchen, lamps, and trade.

The story of this mission is one of growth. Indians kept coming and buildings kept being built. Soon the many people could no longer fit into the tiny chapel.

The biggest and most beautiful church of the missions would be built. A fine stone builder drew up the plans. The church was to be built in the shape of a cross. Everyone wanted to help build it. Men, women, and children all carried stones from several miles away. The yellow stone was called sandstone. The church took nine years to build. A great celebration followed that lasted for two whole days. Many people came, even the governor.

Only six years later, in 1812, an earthquake struck. The dome ceiling came tumbling down. It crashed on top of the people during a church service. Sadly, all forty Indians were killed.

This mission was planned to be built halfway in between the San Diego and San Gabriel missions. It enjoyed twenty years of success. The mission is named for St. John, who was born at Capistrano near Rome, Italy.

TODAY AT THE MISSION

The swallows build their mud nests in the ruins of the stone church. Their flights are famous. Crowds of people gather to watch them. The birds fly South for the winter on October 23rd. Cheering crowds of people welcome them back to the mission every March 19th. They are rarely late.

Father Serra's chapel is still standing. It is the oldest church in California where Father Serra held services. Many art objects from early days can be seen inside. An altar is made of cherry wood and carved by hand. Surrounding it are other religious objects such as wooden statues and crosses. There is an old stone baptismal bowl with a wooden cover. The mud-colored adobe brick walls are four-feet thick. Over the years the bright colors of the Indians' art has become lighter. The walls have been brushed with more paint to make them look like before.

The museum shows objects from the Juaneno Indians' daily lives. Baskets and tools can be found. Among them are fire starters, cutting, and grinding tools. They used the grinding tools: manos, metates, mortars, and pestle in preparing food and medicine.

Walk around the grounds. There is much to see at this mission. A statue of Father Serra and an Indian boy greet visitors as they walk in past the fountain.

The *campanario* or bell tower houses four bells from mission times. The Indian graveyard, soldiers' barracks (rooms), padres' quarters, and workshops can also be seen.

Statue of Father Serra and Indian boy

77

Outdoors look for the *gristmill* used for grinding grain, corn, and crushing olives. The indoor kitchen is where meals were prepared for the padres. The outdoor kitchen was used to cook meals for the Indians.

In the workshop area find the smelter or furnace. This is the oldest metalworks in California. It was used for making locks, keys, iron bars, and other metal objects. Nearby the tanning vats can be seen where the Indians worked the skins of animals into leather goods.

Visitors, artists, and photographers visit the mission. Flowers are in bloom. Young and old people like the green gardens, long adobe hallways, and sparkling fountains. It is one of the most beautiful missions.

Gristmill for grinding corn, grain, and olives

The mission today, front (top) and corridor (bottom)

79

Mission Santa Clara de Asis during mission days

CHAPTER 12

SANTA CLARA DE ASIS

Eighth Mission, founded January 12, 1777

Almost all the missions are named after a saint. This is the first one to be named after a woman. A young woman wanted to live her life dedicated in service to God. Her parents objected. At eighteen, she ran away to live her religious way of life. Saint Claire founded an order (group) of nuns called the Poor Clares.

This mission began slowly but grew into a successful mission. The people at the Santa Clara Mission had to struggle to gain that success.

Lieutenant Moraga, Father Tomas de la Pena, some mission Indians, and soldiers with their families came to start the mission. Father Jose Murguia joined them a few weeks later from Monterey. The soldiers and Indians began constructing buildings. The walls went up slowly with so few people to help.

The local Indians were friendly but hungry. They took some of the Spaniards' mules for food. Soldiers followed them back to their village and fought with them. Soldiers took some of the Indian leaders back to the mission and beat them. Then the Indians did not want to come to the mission.

Sickness spread and many of the Indian children died. Their parents brought their children to be baptized hoping to save them from death.

The weather turned against them. Rain poured down most of the first winter. Water in the Guadalupe River rose higher and higher. It flowed over the top and rushed out, flooding over the buildings. This was not the last time it was to happen. A second time floods washed away buildings. An earthquake hit buildings and crumbled them away again.

The mission had to be moved to different sites many times because of the floods, fires, and earthquakes. Each time the buildings needed to be rebuilt.

A few months after the mission was founded, settlers came. They built the *pueblo* (town) of San Jose across the river from the mission. Problems grew between the settlers and the people at the mission. Cattle wandered back and forth between the two places. Who owned them? Where did mission land end and *pueblo* land begin? Who had the rights to the water from the Guadalupe River? Many arguments needed to be settled.

Rows of trees planted on either side of the road joined the town and the mission. Called *The Alameda*, it stretched four miles long. It helped to ease the problems between the mission and the town. On Sundays men from town drove their families to the mission church in carriages drawn by horses.

The mission grew and prospered inspite of its problems. By 1800 over 1200 Indians lived at the mission. They learned skilled trades. Crops and orchards of fruit and olive trees grew well. Their wheat crop was among the best at any mission. Many thousands of herds of livestock roamed mission land.

One of the reasons the Indians came to the mission was Father Jose Viader. He served the mission for 37 years. His musical talent helped him to train an excellent choir of Indians known throughout the missions.

The padre was a tall, big man with a kind heart. Not all the Indians liked him. One night three Indians crept into his room. They tried to beat him. The padre was so strong he fought them all off and won. He gave them a strict talk on how badly they had acted. Then he forgave them and became their friend.

Another padre named Father Magin Catala lived at the mission for many years. The Indians called him *El Profesta* or the prophet. They believed he could tell the future. He told them Spain would no longer rule the land. He said gold would be found in California. Both things did happen.

TODAY AT THE MISSION

During the good times, the mission lands grew delicious fruit. Orange, palm, and olive trees sway in the wind today. Grapevines grow and red roses bloom in the garden. Though the buildings are gone, many of the original trees and plants once planted by the padres still remain. Heavy rains washed the adobe buildings away. Blazing fires burned down other buildings in the early 1900s.

Back in 1850, Father John Nobili tried to start a college in some of the buildings. He was able to get back some of mission land sold after secularization. The school he started has now grown into the University of Santa Clara. It is the only mission to become part of a university. It is also the oldest university in California. Since that time many buildings have been added. A new church has been built to look like the old one. A wooden cross stands in front of the church dating from mission days.

A museum, the De Saisset Art Gallery and Museum, displays objects from mission times. Among them is an old metal bell given to the mission by the King of Spain. It was carried all the way from Spain by ship to California. Father Pena's diary or notebook in which he recorded his life at the mission is kept in a glass case. The mission register tells how many animals, Indians, and goods the mission recorded for each year.

The mission site, church replica, and museum are located on the University of Santa Clara campus in the town of Santa Clara.

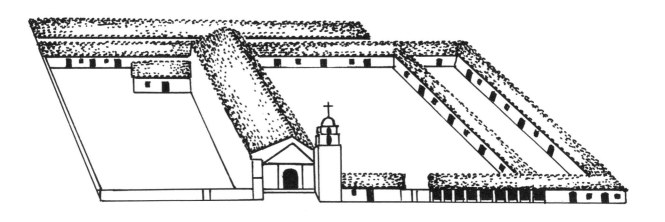

Mission San Buenaventura during mission days

CHAPTER 13

SAN BUENAVENTURA

Ninth Mission founded March 31, 1782

On Easter Sunday, Father Serra raised the wooden cross and blessed it. Under a brushwood shelter the first church service took place.

At last San Buenaventura had been founded! For many years it was put off. The San Gabriel Mission Indians fought against the soldiers because they had been unfairly treated. The governor sent more soldiers to protect the mission. Then there were not enough soldiers to protect the padres to found a new mission.

When the Spaniards came, they found the Chumash Indians to be very clever and friendly. They lived in houses made of tule grass and slept on beds filled with straw. The men were skilled at making large canoes from wood. The women were known for the beauty of their basketmaking.

The Spaniards watched as the Indians made their houses in a cone shape. The Indians picked strong tree branches and cut them down for poles. They stuck the poles deep in the ground in the shape of a circle. Then they dug out the earth inside it. Bending the tops of the poles, they tied them together with leather strips. Women wove mats of grass for the outside of the hut. The mats were joined to the poles to form the walls. The top was left open so smoke from the fire could come out.

The Indians quickly accepted Christianity and helped the Spaniards build the mission. Their buildings could not stand up to the strong shaking of earthquakes. The earthquake of 1812 hit, and the bell tower fell down. A huge wave called a tidal wave swept close to the mission. It nearly washed it away. All over California buildings crumbled. Many people were killed.

The earth at the mission was dry. It needed water for crops to grow. The Indians made clay pipes to bring water to the land. This water system stretched for seven miles to the mission and flowed out of a stone horse head. The Indians called it *caballo*, which is Spanish for horse. It allowed them to grow some unusual crops. Bananas, sugar cane, figs, and coconuts grew plentifully on the land. They grew the usual crops too and became a productive mission in farming. Many livestock grazed on the land.

By 1816 over a thousand Indians came to live at the mission. The mission Indians were not allowed to trade with Indians who were not Christians. The padres feared they would go back to their villages and their old ways. Mojave Indians, non-Christians, came to the mission to trade. The padres found out about it. They ordered the Indians thrown in jail. The angry Indians fought with the soldiers. Several Indians were killed. This event caused bad feelings among all the Indians.

Bouchard, the pirate, raided the land in 1818. People at the mission buried the statues and valuables. Then they fled to the mountains and hid. They waited until the pirates had gone.

After the United States took over California, the mission became a Catholic church. One priest decided to paint it. He covered up the beautiful Indian paintings on the walls. He took away art and objects from early days. It is too bad only the adobe walls and a side door are all that is left of the Indians' work.

TODAY AT THE MISSION

The church and its gardens are what is left of the mission. Inside, the restored paintings of the 14 Stations of the Cross hang from the walls. Beams and tiles are original. Services are held in the parish church today. This mission is the last one to be founded by Father Serra.

A small museum displays Chumash baskets, farming tools, and other artifacts. Wooden bells are unqiue among them. This is the only mission to use wooden bells instead of iron. Religious objects and many vestments or clothes the padres wore for church services can be seen.

Next to the mission parking lot visit the Archaeological Interpretive Center. Outdoors, it reveals mission foundations, an earth oven, a well, and part of the mission water system. The model of a Chumash boat stands outside the museum building. The Albinger Archaeological Museum includes many artifacts discovered here. Shell beads, arrowheads, bone whistles, medallions, pottery on display were used by the Indians.

Down the street a block is the Ventura County History Museum. It is an excellent museum to learn about California history. Visitors will find a mission model; early photographs; art; farm equipment; and tools of Indian, Mexican, and American settler periods. Visitors will enjoy seeing all these fascinating places within a block of each other in downtown Ventura.

Mission San Buenaventura before rebuilding (top) and today (bottom)

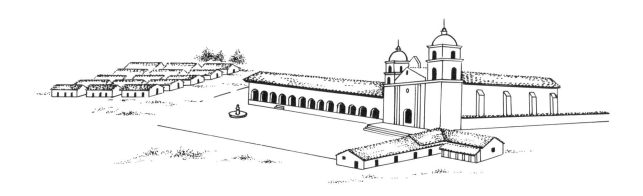

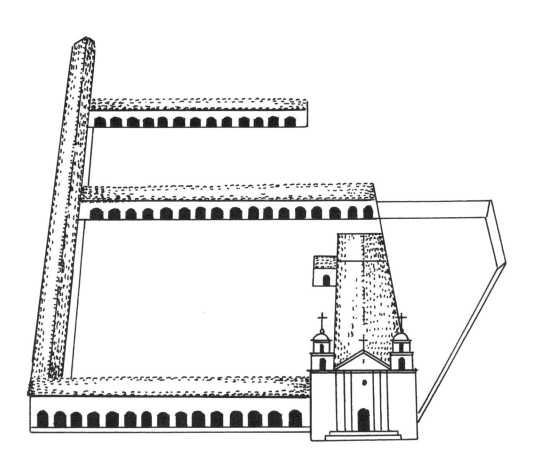

Mission Santa Barbara Mission during mission days

CHAPTER 14

SANTA BARBARA

Tenth Mission, founded December 4, 1786

Father Serra was happy and excited! A fort at Santa Barbara soon would be built. Though permission had not come, a mission was planned to be built near it. Father Serra joined the soldiers on their journey. He chose the land for the mission and blessed it. But the government did not give permission. Several more years of waiting would pass before this would happen. Father Serra did not know that Governor Felipe de Neve was against the way the mission system was run.

He wanted another plan. He thought they should send one padre instead of two. The padre would live alone in a house built next to the chapel. A few soldiers would guard him. No mission was to be built where the Indians would come to live. The padre would visit them in their villages. Here he would teach them about Christianity.

This system was tried in Colorado the year before and failed. Many padres were killed by Indians. Father Serra fought against the governor's plan. He would not let this same thing happen in California. Years later permission for the founding of the new mission came. Father Fermin de Lasuen dedicated it. He left Fathers Antonio Paterna and Cristobal Oramas to run it.

Only one out of three Indians became Christians in early California. The Chumash and Canalino Indians of this area welcomed the Spaniards. They helped them build adobe buildings. Many clung to their old ways and built grass huts to live in at the Indian village. Later they lived in adobes too.

Orange and olive trees grew in long rows called orchards. A water system brought water to the rich fields of wheat, barley, corn, beans, and peas. It brought it to the mission where it poured out of a stone fountain shaped like a bear's head. The water filled up into a basin (tub) where the women washed clothes. They spent many hours talking with each other as they scrubbed their families' clothes clean.

Livestock multiplied and became important to the mission. Thousands of cattle and sheep grazed on pasture land. Trades developed at the mission. The Indians built a church, kitchen, storerooms, living quarters, a tannery, and shops. Indians kept coming until in 1807 about 1,700 Indians lived at the mission. Three churches needed to be built at different times. Each was built larger than the one before.

In 1812 an earthquake hit and damaged most the buildings. Several years later a stone mason from Mexico came to build the stone church. It was planned by Father Antonio Ripoll. Before the padre built it, he turned through the pages of many books. What did he know about building? Not very much. He decided to learn. He designed it to have two tall bell towers and be made out of yellow sandstone. Stonemason, Jose Ramirez and his Indian helpers, completed the actual work. It took five years to build.

In 1820, the church was completed. They held a festival (party) when it was finished. It lasted for three days! The church measured 179 feet long and 38 feet wide with walls built 6 feet thick.

On February 21, 1824 an Indian rider came with news from Santa Ines Mission. A soldier had beaten an Indian without good reason. The Indians were fighting against the soldiers. Would the Santa Barbara Indians like to join the fight?

The mission Indians talked among themselves. The soldiers punished them too harshly. They laughed at them. They brought sicknesses that many Indians died from. Life at the mission seemed stricter everyday. There were so many rules to follow. The padres made them work so hard. Yes, they decided, they would join the attack.

Quickly, the Indian men sent the women and children off into the hills for safety. Then they attacked the mission. Bullets flew through the air. Indians and soldiers fought with each other. Finally, the fighting calmed down and the Indians escaped. They ran up into the hills to join their families. They took up with the warlike Tulare Indians. Only a few old Indians stayed behind.

What was a mission without Indians? Nothing. The padres had no one to teach Christianity to. The work came to a stop. The padre visited the Indians and begged them to come back. After four months, many went back. Others did not ever want to.

TODAY AT THE MISSION

The mission sits high on a hill overlooking the beach town of Santa Barbara. The design of the building is beautiful and unusual. It looks like old Greek and Roman buildings.

The sandstone church still stands. Over the years, the many earthquakes that have shaken California have weakened it. This is the only mission that has always had a padre living here to look after it. This is why the buildings are in good condition. Many of the paintings inside are two hundred years old. Several of the padres of the mission lay buried underneath the floor. Bells ring only on Sundays to call people who still worship in the church. Outside the church leading to the cemetery notice the two human skulls and crossbones above the doorway.

In the graveyard over four thousand Indians are buried. Among them is Juana Maria. She was known as "the woman of San Nicolas Island." Did you ever read the fiction book, *Island of the Blue Dolphins* by Scott O'Dell? The story was based on her life.

An excellent museum shows old photographs of the mission. A display recreates what a missionary bedroom looked like. The bed is made of a wooden frame with an animal skin stretched across it. Displays of Chumash art, trades, and a kitchen can also help the visitor understand what it was like to live here.

It is fun to walk around the garden. In front can you find the fountain and basin where Indian women washed the clothes?

The ruins of the water system, a mill, tanning vats, a storage reservoir can be seen near the mission. This water system is considered the best built of the missions.

The mission buildings in more modern times have been used for a high school, junior college, and a school for priests.

Santa Barbara is called the *queen* of the missions because it is one of the most beautifully designed. It is one of the most important centers for mission and California history in the United States.

Mission Santa Barbara today (top) and the ruins of the water system (bottom)

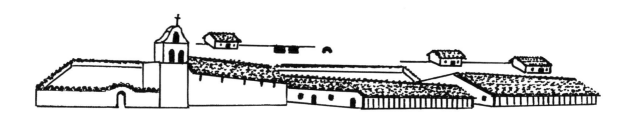

Mission La Purisima Concepcion during mission days

CHAPTER 15

LA PURISIMA CONCEPCION

Eleventh Mission, founded December 8, 1787

Success of a mission depended on many things. Good land and plenty of water were necessary for growing crops. There should be friendly Indians and kind, wise padres. Skilled trades needed to be learned and developed at the mission. Many herds of animals must be raised to help feed the people. La Purisima had all of these.

The land was carefully chosen. It was located in a valley near a river. Father Lasuen planted the cross. The founding of this mission had been put off by Governor Neve.

It began as a prosperous mission. In the orchards, golden pears hung from the many fruit trees. Green and red grapes spilled over grapevines. From the grapes, the Indians made wine. This mission was famous for its fruits.

More than a thousand Indians came to live here. They made important products for the mission in the workshops. Candles and soap were made from tallow. Rough cloth and blankets were woven from wool. They skillfully cut and shaped leather into saddles and harnesses for horses and shoes for the people.

The beginning of their troubles started with the earthquake of 1812. All over California the ground shook. The walls of the mission swayed. Cracks opened in the walls. The people were afraid. After the first quake, the padres were looking over the damage. Just then another quake hit. The buildings shook even harder. This time they fell down in ruins. Heavy rains followed, washing away the broken ruins.

95

Their problems never stopped. The land dried out when the rain did not come. Crops failed. A very cold winter killed hundreds of sheep. A fire burned down many Indian huts. Measles, smallpox, and other sicknesses killed many Indians. Father Mariano Payeras, who had served at the mission for 20 years, died. The Indians felt sad and discouraged.

At this time the war between Mexico and Spain was going on. It brought hardship to their lives. No supplies came to the mission. The Indians had to make more goods. They worked even harder than before. They had little freedom. The soldiers treated them worse. The government would not pay the soldiers anymore for their jobs. This was because of the war. The soldiers often took their problems out on the Indians.

What else could go wrong? News came from Mission Santa Ines of the Indian attack on that mission. The Chumash Indians at La Pursima were ready. They had hidden away food, supplies, and guns. They attacked their own mission and took charge of it for a month.

More soldiers came to fight against them. They arrived from the *presidio* at Monterey. Another battle began. Over 100 soldiers fought the Indians for two and a half hours. Finally, the Indians had to give up. The Indians who had not wanted to fight against the mission had hidden in the mountains. They came back after the fighting was over mainly because they had nowhere else to go.

Later, the mission lands were sold for $1,100 in 1845. Through the years, the mission changed hands many times. It became a stable for animals. In the days of the Old West, it became a saloon and a hideout for outlaws.

TODAY AT THE MISSION

Mission ranches and farms are gone. Only a few walls were standing when the State of California took it over. Now they own it and keep it running. It is one of the few missions built in a straight line not in a quadrangle shape.

This mission is one of the most fully rebuilt ones. The setting is rural and there is much to see. Stepping across the bridge is like stepping back into history.

Many outdoor and indoor workshops have been rebuilt and can be seen today. A pottery shop shows where the Indians made tiles for floor, roof, and water channel pipes. Among the shops include a blacksmith's, weaving, leather, and carpentry ones. A sign tells in the soap workshop how the soap for the mission was made. The clay pipes from the water channel wind down from the hills.

The church, quarters' building, chapel, dining, residence, guest rooms, and the *monjerio* or girls' dormitory can be explored. Walk through the Indian cemetery.

Animals are fenced in pens outside. They remind the visitors of the many animals that once roamed the lands. This mission gives visitors a picture of what life must have been like during mission days. It is located near the city of Lompoc.

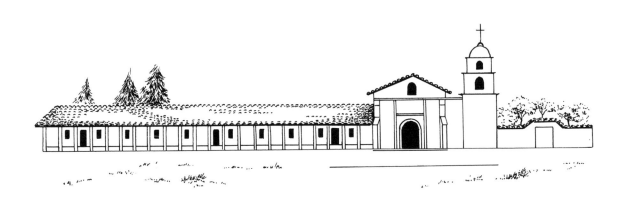

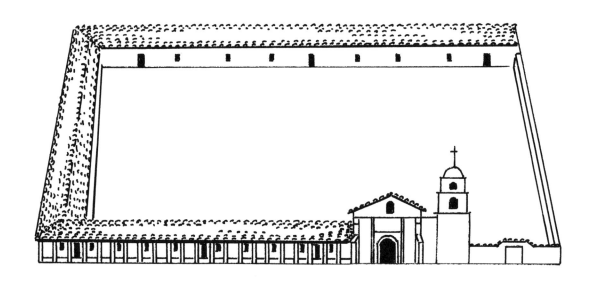

Mission Santa Cruz during mission days

CHAPTER 16

SANTA CRUZ

Twelfth Mission, founded August 28, 1791

The sun shone down and sparkled on the clear, blue water. Indian children ran into the waves. They splashed each other. On the shore other children played their favorite games. Some spun tops made from acorns gathered near the mission. Two raced each other to see who could run the fastest.

The view from the mission was beautiful. It overlooked the water. The land chosen seemed perfect. The good weather, rich soil, and plentiful water made this an ideal site. Trees in the forest and stone nearby could be used for building the mission.

The early years passed happily by. Grains, fruits, and vegetables grew on the lands. Many Indians came to live at the mission. A new church was begun in 1793 and finished the following year. By 1796 the Indians numbered around 500. A gristmill, granary, and weaving room were added to the many other buildings. Troubled times would change this success.

A rainstorm damaged the church in 1799 so badly it needed to be rebuilt. The flooding it caused killed animals and destroyed crops.

One night an Indian asked a padre, Father Quintana, to visit a sick Indian. Father Quintana was in the orchard. He did not want to go back to the mission to wake up a soldier to go with him. He followed the Indian. On his way home, he was attacked and killed by several other Indians. The Indians were punished, but they said the padre had treated them badly.

The biggest problem was yet to come. Settlers came to live across the river in a new town called Branciforte in 1818. This town caused many problems for the mission. Some of the people who came were dishonest. Once fear of pirates spread to Santa Cruz. Monterey nearby had been attacked and set on fire in 1818 by Bouchard and his pirates. Would the pirates come to Santa Cruz?

Governor Pablo de Sola ordered Father Olbes, the priest, and the Indians to leave the mission. They followed orders and fled to Mission Soledad. There they would be safe.

The settlers were told to hide the mission valuables. The pirates never came, but some of the settlers did. Father Olbes and the Indians returned to find all of the mission's valuables stolen. The settlers had not only stolen them but damaged the inside of the church.

Father Olbes grew angry! He reported the theft at once to the governor. The people never returned them. Father Olbes threatened to leave the mission, but the church would not let him.

This was not the mission's last problems with the people of Branciforte. The town became a place for gambling, thievery, and drunkenness. This was too close to the mission and proved to be a poor influence on the Indians. Many of the settlers did not want to work in the fields or raise herds of animals as they had agreed to do. Instead, they hired mission Indians to work for them. Indians left the mission to do this.

Through these troubled times farming and herds of animals grew. Many Indians became discouraged with mission life and left. By 1831 there were only about 300 Indians left. The mission could not go on without them.

Mexico came to power and sent an administrator or leader to run it. He divided it up among the settlers. A series of earthquakes in 1857 destroyed the church. By the time this mission was put up for sale, no one wanted to buy it.

TODAY AT THE MISSION

What began as a perfect mission ended as a total failure. Fewer Indians lived here than at any other mission in California. Today, a new mission chapel has been built, though smaller than the old one. A few paintings, priests' robes, statues, and religious objects are most of what remain from mission days. They can be found in the chapel, gift shop, and a small museum off the gift shop.

Santa Cruz means sacred cross in Spanish. Its name stands for the symbol of Christianity. Mission lands and the town of Branciforte are now part of the seaside community of Santa Cruz.

Across the street from the chapel, another church stands tall built in a Gothic style. This church was built on the original site of the first mission church.

Nearby at the end of School Street is an old adobe building. It is thought to have been the soldiers' living quarters of the old mission.

Mission Nuestra Senora de la Soledad during mission days

CHAPTER 17

NUESTRA SENORA DE LA SOLEDAD

Thirteenth Mission, founded October 9, 1791

Thirteen is an unlucky number people sometimes believe. Soledad is the thirteenth mission to be founded. Was it unlucky? Why did it fail?

The story of the mission began many years before it was founded. Captain Portola and Father Juan Crespi came and camped here for the night. They were looking for land on which to build another mission.

An Indian wandered by. He spoke to them. He said the same word over and over again. It sounded like *soledad*. The visitors knew the word meant *loneliness* in Spanish. They looked around them at the flat, treeless land. No one else was in sight. They agreed with the Indian. It was a lonely place.

Twenty-two years later another padre came. Father Lasuen founded the mission. Few Indians lived around here. Mission sites were usually chosen near a large number of Indian villages.

This mission needed to be built for another reason too. Many people walked in the days of early California. Others rode horseback. All the travelers needed a safe resting place. This mission would be a day's travel between the San Antonio and San Carlos Missions.

It took time to build up the number of Indians at the mission. With so few people to help, the buildings went up slowly. The people worked as hard as they could.

The mission experienced many troubles. Farming did not do well. The people brought water from the Salinas and Arroyo Seco Rivers through clay pipes. Still, the crops did not grow. Sometimes too little rain fell. At other times it poured down. When this happened, the two rivers flooded their banks. It ruined crops and destroyed buildings three different times.

The Indians learned how to build irrigation systems. The herds of sheep, horses, and cattle grew. This helped to feed the mission Indians.

The bad weather and troubles made this a mission where most padres did not want to come. The rooms turned cold in the winter. They baked in the summer heat. A sickness called *the Plague* killed many Indians. Many left to find a better life.

All these problems placed a heavy load on the padres. They came and went. They asked to go to other missions. No padre stayed longer than four years. They did not find happiness here.

Other padres wanted to help. Padre Ibanez came to the mission. The Indians liked him because he was gentle and good to them. He taught them to read and write. He took care of them when they were sick. He loved and respected them.

Another padre came later named Father Vicente Francisco Sarria. He hoped to change the troubles of the mission. He loved the Indians and tried to keep the mission going. The crops failed and there was little food. He often gave his share to the Indians. Sadly, he died of hunger. The Indians carried him to San Antonio Mission and left the Soledad Mission. With the kind padre gone, the Indians did not want to stay.

In 1841 the buildings and 42 acres of mission land were sold for $800. It was returned to the Catholic church when the United States took over.

TODAY AT THE MISSION

For one hundred years, nothing was done to protect and care for the buildings. They fell down, and the roof was sold. All that was left of the mission was the front part of the chapel. Now this little white chapel and the padres' rooms have been rebuilt.

Inside the church stands the statue of Our Lady of the Sorrows. The padres' rooms house a museum and gift shop. The bell hanging near the chapel is left from mission days. The ruins of the quadrangle can be seen.

Mission Nuestra Senora de la Soledad today

The statue of Our Lady of Sorrows inside the chapel

105

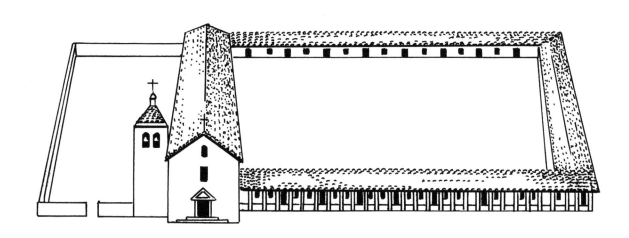

Mission San Jose during mission days

CHAPTER 18

SAN JOSE

Fourteenth Mission, founded June 11, 1797

Another rest stop was needed. The Indians on this land attacked the soldiers and travelers riding through. Maybe if a mission could be built, they would become friendlier. The land was chosen two years before they built the mission.

What should it be called? Everyone thought up a different name. Father Antonio Daniti who chose it called it San Francisco Solano for a stream he named nearby. The Indians called it Oroysom. The governor of the territory (land) called it *The Alameda.*

The governor in Mexico decided he would get to choose the name since he was the highest government leader. He said it would be called San Carlos Borromeo. Quickly, someone told him there already was a California mission with that name! To cover his embarrassment, he gave it a new name, San Jose. It is named for St. Joseph.

The founding ceremony must have been quite a sight to see. They tried to interest the Indians so they would come to the mission. Everyone dressed in their best clothes. Soldiers, padres, and Indians came from other missions. Father Lasuen began the ceremony. He sprinkled holy water on the land and blessed it. A wooden cross was planted in the ground. The soldiers raised the flag of Spain. They fired their guns. The worship service then took place. Many Indians watched.

The nearby Santa Clara Mission gave the mission many animals. They drove cattle, horses, mules, oxen, sheep, and bulls along the trail. Mission Dolores sent them animals too. Older missions usually gave what they could to new missions just starting out. Soldiers began to build the first buildings. The mission was off to a good start.

Not many Indians came. They liked their lives and the freedom to roam the land. One adult Indian woman did come to be baptized. Fathers Barcenilla and Merino were new padres. How did they baptize someone? They did not know. Quickly, they sent a messenger to Mission Santa Clara. Father Magin de Catala came to help. He showed them how and wrote the woman's new name, Josefa, in the baptism book.

As time went on, the Indians changed their minds. They came from miles away to live at the mission. They helped to build the church, sleeping quarters, workshops, and other rooms for the mission.

Though the mission was successful, many outbreaks of fighting took place. Once in 1805 an Indian ran to Father Cueva to tell him of sick, runaway Indians that needed his help. He begged the priest to come. A group of soldiers and a few mission Indians went with the padre into the mountains. On the way they were attacked by hostile Indians. Many were killed.

Another time in 1828 a mission Indian named Estanislao ran away. He did not like the mission. He wandered among the runaway Indians talking and planning against the mission. One night they attacked the mission. Soldiers jumped out of their beds and grabbed their guns. They fired at the Indians. The Indians shot back but lost in the end. The padre forgave them. Estanislao and many others came back to live at the mission. He is the Indian for whom Stanislaus County in California is named.

This mission grew to be the most successful mission in northern California. In 1831 1,886 Indian converts lived at the mission. They developed trades here, though farming was more important. Vegetables, fruits, and crops grew plentifully. During this same year around 12,000 cattle, 13,000 sheep, and 13,000 horses grazed on mission lands.

Fathers Duran and Fortuni are among the reasons for the success of this mission. Father Duran served the mission for 27 years. He was a good leader and a talented musician. He showed the Indians how to play musical instruments. The Indians loved music and singing. They practiced in a group of thirty people called an orchestra. Their musical talent made them famous. People came from miles away to hear them play.

The mission was sold in 1845 but later left alone by its owners. H.C. Smith operated a store here during the Gold Rush. The sleepy town became a busy center for supplies to the southern mines. It was used as a saloon and a hotel. People stole the mission treasures over the years. Buildings crumbled and fell down. The 1868 earthquake along the Hayward Fault destroyed the adobe church and many other buildings.

TODAY AT THE MISSION

Today, the mission is a small reminder of a once busy community. Recently, a reconstructed adobe church was completed in 1985. This was done through the efforts of a group of people who formed the Committee for the Restoration of the Mission San Jose and the Diocese of Oakland. It took 150,000 bricks to rebuild the church. It is 126 feet long and 30 feet wide. The walls are 4 to 5 feet thick, and it is beautifully decorated inside.

The padre's living quarters is now a museum. It houses an excellent exhibit showing the Ohlone Indian history and culture. They have lived on this land since before mission times and still do. A padre's room, display of religious objects, and a slide show about the mission can also be viewed.

The mission is located in the city of Fremont, 15 miles from the city of San Jose.

Rebuilt church at Mission San Jose

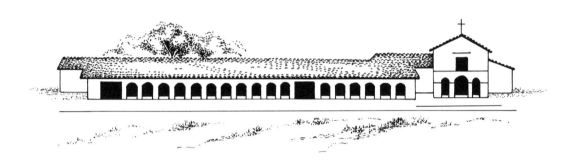

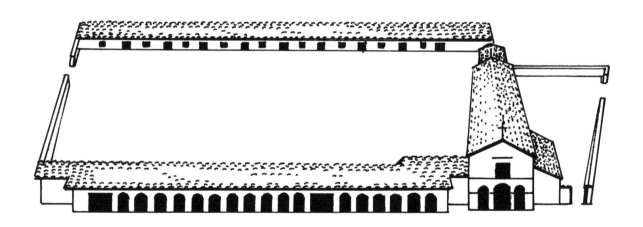

Mission San Juan Bautista during mission days

CHAPTER 19

SAN JUAN BAUTISTA

Fifteenth Mission, founded June 24, 1797

Little did the padres know where they had built their mission. It sat on top of the biggest earthquake fault in California! A fault is a weak spot in the earth. The land cracks and the earth moves back and forth. This one is called the San Andreas Fault. Many quakes shook this land and the mission.

Father Arroyo de la Cuesta tried hard to interest the Indians in coming to the mission. He learned over twelve languages. In church he preached in seven different languages. He wanted them to understand the new religion. The friendly Indians did come. They helped the padre build a church and mission buildings.

The mission was successful from the beginning. Thirty-six acres of pear and apple orchards were planted. The Indians raised thousands of cattle and sheep. Crops of wheat and corn grew well, and trades were developed.

Father Cuesta liked to give the Indians who came to the mission new Christian names. He gave them names of famous people in history. He named them after kings like Alexander and great leaders like Plato.

The Indians kept on coming. Men, women, and children squeezed into the church. So many came that a bigger church needed to be built. The padres made plans in 1812. The church took a long time to build. When it was completed, it could hold 1,000 Indians, but by then times had changed. Many Indians had died or left the mission. There no longer were enough Indians to fill it. The people had to put up a wall to make it smaller.

111

Everyone enjoyed music at the mission. One of the padres knew all about music. Father Estevan Tapis even wrote his own music. Singing voices filled the church. The padre used a special way to teach the Indians music. He colored the notes in red, white, black, and yellow. Each person learned their part by following their own color. Music became an important part of their lives. Once it saved them.

Unfriendly Indians attacked the mission. The padre ran to the barrel organ and began to play. Beautiful sounds came from the organ pipes. The padre's idea worked. It surprised the attacking Indians. What was this strange object? They listened to the sounds that came like magic from the wooden box. They forgot about fighting and wanted to stay.

This rich mission boasted of many Indians living here, herds of animals, and good farming. Time brought this to an end.

TODAY AT THE MISSION

The earthquake damage to the building can be seen on the side of the walls. Steel and concrete beams strengthen the building for future earthquakes. Today the mission church, padres' dining room, *convento*, and cemetery can be seen. A bell tower stands to the right of the church. Two of the bells are original from mission days.

The church is one of the largest of the mission chain. Inside it is shaped in an L. The walls have been repainted with Indian-style designs and brightly decorate the walls and ceilings.

The wooden altar was carved by hand. A sailor named Thomas Doak painted it in blue and red. He had left his ship. Another worker offered to paint it for $.75 a day. Doak needed a place to stay and food to eat. He painted it for free. Doak liked California so well, he decided to stay. This made him the first American to settle here.

The *convento* houses a museum and gift shop inside. In the museum is a restored kitchen where Indians prepared food for the mission. A barrel organ is also on display.

Outside behind the church is a building that was the mission's jail. On the other side of the cemetery wall, visitors can see the famous San Andreas fault. This is the most active earthquake fault in California.

Today the mission (below) stands in a plaza. A hotel, two adobe houses, and a stable share the plaza. All look like they did in the times of early California. They are part of the San Juan Bautista State Historic Park.

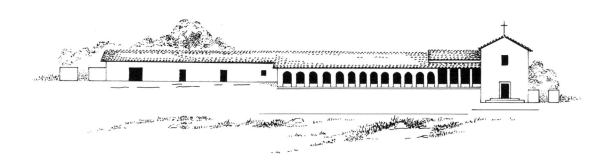

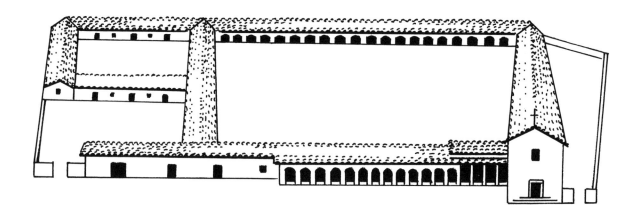

Mission San Miguel Arcangel during mission days

114

CHAPTER 20

SAN MIGUEL ARCANGEL

Sixteenth Mission, founded July 25, 1797

The Salinian Indians eagerly waited for the day when the padres would come. This was unusual. Many of their friends and relatives lived happily in other missions. They heard good things about the missions. The expedition came. By the end of the first day, the padres had bapized fifteen Indian children.

Buildings went up fast with the willing Indians helping. People knew more about building now than when missions were first established. Other missions sent the animals and supplies needed to begin the mission. Several Indian families came from other missions to help.

A smooth beginning ended with trouble from their padre, Father Antonio Horra. He did not like missionary life. He grew lonely so far away from the other padres and a town. The heat and numerous ants bothered him. Each day grew worse. He hated it more and could not fit in. Then he started doing strange things. He fired guns and scared off some of the Indians. The padre went insane and was sent back to Mexico.

One month after the mission was founded, Father Juan Martin came to take Father Horra's place. Father Martin stayed for twenty-seven years. It was during this time most of the buildings were constructed.

A fire broke out in 1806. The storehouses burned to the ground. The mission's supply of wheat was destroyed. Workshops burned down so the Indians could not make what they needed. Nearby missions helped them. They sent all the supplies they could spare to help the mission.

Life at San Miguel soon returned to normal. They could start building again. During a two-year time, the Indians built a carpentry shop, a warehouse, living quarters, a weaving room, and other buildings. Roofs were now built of tile and would not burn. The Indians at this mission became so good at making tiles that they were known for trading them with other missions. Between 1808-9 they made 36,000 tiles!

The number of Indians grew to one thousand. That was before the war between Mexico and Spain brought hard times. There was not enough food to feed the Indians. Father Ramon left in 1841. He had lived there for forty-seven years.

San Miguel was the last mission to be sold in July of 1846. It was bought only a few days before the United States took over California. William Reed and Petronillo Rios bought the mission. Reed moved his family into the mission and opened a store. Travelers passing through stopped for several days to rest. Reed was not wise. He liked to talk about his money. He told them about the money he had made from selling cattle and sheep and the gold from the mines. The greedy visitors robbed him and killed everyone at the mission.

Later the mission was used as a saloon, dance hall, storeroom, and living quarters.

TODAY AT THE MISSION

The mission looks similar to mission days. Arches of different heights and widths rise along the corridor of the *convento*. This is unlike most missions, which are mainly the same height. Outside in the garden grow a variety of cacti.

A weaving display shows a spinning wheel and loom used by the Indians

The museum and displays are excellent at this mission. Visitors can experience what it might have been like to live here. The dining room, the padre's sleeping room, a living room, ruins of the wine vat, and the padre's kitchen show scenes from early days. A wool-drying rack, spinning wheel, and weaving loom recreate how the Indians made wool into clothing.

Outside, the church is plain but colorful inside. It is 144 feet long, 27 feet wide, and 40 feet high. The bright decorations were painted by a Mexican artist, Esteban Munros, and his Indian helpers. The carpentry and wood are beautiful. The statue in the center is of St. Michael, for whom the mission is named. This church has the best preserved interior of any of the missions.

The mission is located in the town of San Miguel seven miles north of Paso Robles.

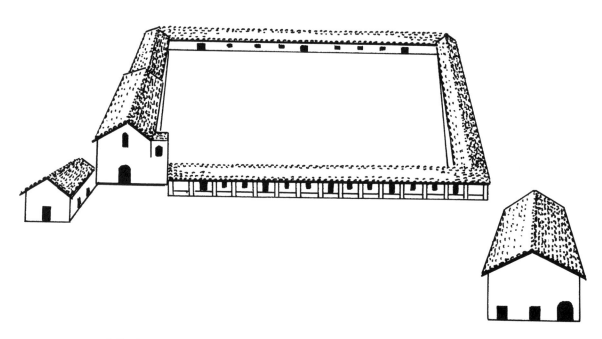

Mission San Fernando Rey de Espana during mission days

CHAPTER 21

SAN FERNANDO REY

Seventeenth Mission, founded September 8, 1797

The padres founded four missions the year this mission was established. San Fernando became one of the largest missions. Older missions gave them a good start. They provided them with horses, mules, cattle, sheep, and oxen. The herds grew bigger. Cattle-raising became their most important activity. Many Indians were needed to herd, brand, and raise the cattle. The year 1819 turned out to be the best year for raising livestock. Cattle, sheep, goats, pigs, horses, and mules totalled 21,745 animals.

The Indians learned the trades. The blacksmith pounded metal into tools, plows, branding irons, and fancy ironwork. He made horseshoes for the mules and horses at the mission. This mission became known for its fine ironwork.

Carpentry, weaving, leathermaking, adobe, tile, and soapmaking also became important trades at the mission.

The Indians were also famous for their grapes. The padres brought the vines all the way from Spain to plant. They grew well in the good weather. Indians picked the plump, juicy grapes. They hauled them by oxcart from the fields to the mission. Then they threw them in pits called vats.

After washing their feet, they climbed on top of the grapes. They squished them with their feet. Juice poured out of the bottom of the vat from a wooden pipe. They gathered and stored the juice in oxhides in the cellar. There it turned into wine. Later they used wooden barrels to hold the wine. The wine was used for many things. They needed it for church services, to drink, and for medicine. It could be traded with the outside world and other missions.

Hard times came upon this mission as with the rest. Their lives became difficult during the war. If only the soldiers had earned their own living. They could have planted crops and hunted for game, but they did not. They depended on the Indians to feed and make them what they needed.

Many government leaders lived here. The famous Governor Pio Pico lived here. He was against the mission system and sold the missions when Mexico took over. John Fremont, an American explorer of the West also stayed at this mission.

Gold was found here on March 9, 1842 in what is now Placerita Canyon by Francisco Lopez, the administrator of the mission. He was rounding up stray horses and stopped to rest under a tree. With his knife, he dug up wild onions from the ground. He found gold dust too! Many people, mainly from Los Angeles to Santa Barbara, rushed to the spot to look for gold. After a few years, the excitement and the gold ran out. This strike was small compared to the California Gold Rush that was to follow in 1848.

TODAY AT THE MISSION

Paintings and photographs of the mission have many stories to tell. A mission Indian painted other Indians as they worked in the fields gathering grapes.

A painting of Saint Francis of Asisi hangs in the mission. This painting was almost lost. A man saw it first as a sign, "hay for sale," the sign read. The man stopped to look at the sign. He turned it over. This painting was on the other side. He gave it back to the mission.

The books in the library cover many subjects. Books on farming, building, geography, and religion stand on shelves. Others explain skilled crafts and trades. The daily lives of the people depended on the information found in these books.

In the museum visitors can see displays of the mission, pottery, and a good collection of mission baskets. Workshops show carpentry, pottery, saddle and blacksmith shops, and the weaving room.

The *convento* took thirteen years to build and is famous for its twenty-one Roman arches. Inside, don't miss the wine cellar and vat where the Indians turned grapes into wine.

Look for holes cut in the large mission doors. The cats ran in and out chasing rats. When rats were eating the mission's grain, the padres borrowed cats from the San Gabriel Mission. The cats did a good job of catching the rats.

Today, houses of the San Fernando Valley are built around the old mission.

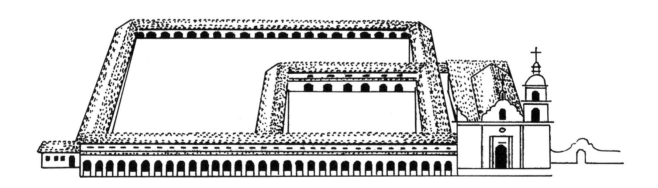

Mission San Luis Rey de Francia during mission days

CHAPTER 22

SAN LUIS REY DE FRANCIA

Eighteenth Mission, founded June 13, 1789

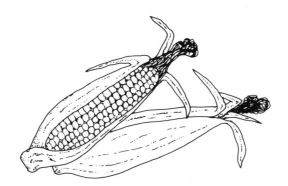

Birds sang from their trees in the gardens. Pear, apple, and peach trees grew tall. The first pepper tree planted in California shaded this mission. In the fields the Luiseno Indians planted wheat, corn, and beans every year. They gathered a large crop of grain. Only the San Gabriel Mission grew more crops.

They raised more livestock than any other mission. Their herds reached 27,000 head of cattle, 26,000 sheep, and several thousand horses.

As time passed, they added many buildings. Three thousand Indians came to the mission. More Indians lived here than at any other mission.

The padre built the church in the shape of a cross. The tall bell tower served as a lookout to warn them of strangers. Indians waved flags to workers in the fields. This told them how many sheep and cattle should be brought to the mission the following day.

Inside the church was a small chapel in the corner. Indians came here to pray for their dead.

Father Antonio Peyri lived at the mission for thirty-four years. He was a kind man whom the Indians liked. A large part of its success was because he ran the mission well. He helped to build up the production of the workshops.

When the Mexican government took over, they told the padre to leave. They said he would have to go back to Spain. He loved the Indians and did not want to have to say goodbye. Late at night he left when everyone was asleep. When the Indians discovered the padre gone, they followed him. They caught up with him and begged him to return. He knew he could not. From the ship, he sadly waved goodbye.

Father Peyri still hoped he could help the Indians. Two Indian boys traveled with him to Spain. He sent them to school. One of them, Pablo Tac, wanted to become a priest. He wrote down the story of his life in a book. This is the only known record to be written by a mission Indian.

This was the most successful of all the missions. After the padre left, it decayed rapidly. Crops, livestock, and mission goods were stolen. Governor Pio Pico sold it for $2,437 to relatives. The Indians went to live in the hills and nearby valleys.

Mission San Luis Rey before rebuilding

124

TODAY AT THE MISSION

Displays at this mission show the daily lives of the people who lived here. The padre's room is plain and simple. A wooden bed is one of the few pieces of furniture. A wool blanket rests at the foot. Above it hangs a wooden cross carved by Indians. Beside it hangs the padre's gray robe and wide-brimmed hat he wore everyday. A water pitcher made of clay he used to wash his face.

On the wall of the kitchen hang many metal pots used for cooking. The brick ovens are not used anymore. Once the Indians packed them with wood and lit them to make a fire. Meals for the mission were cooked here. A large, flat stone and a smaller round one were used for grinding corn and grain.

A candle display shows how pieces of string were hung on a wheel. The candlemaker poured melted tallow on each string. Then he turned the wheel and started the next one. He let the tallow cool and poured on more until it was finished. They were used to light the church and rooms of the mission.

The weaving display is fascinating. Can you picture an Indian woman sitting at the wooden loom weaving a blanket?

At the time of the Mexican War, the U.S. military stayed at the mission. In 1893 the rebuilding of the mission was started. Today, it is well restored but not nearly as large as the six acres of buildings that once stood. The ruins of a sunken garden and *lavenderia* is located in front of the mission. Clothes were washed by the Indians here. This area is currently being restored.

San Luis Rey is called the *king* of the missions. The name fits because this is the largest of all the missions. It was named for King Louis IX of France who fought in the Crusades. The front of the building is beautiful with its thirty-two columns. It is located 30 miles north of San Diego in Oceanside.

Mission Santa Ines during mission days

126

CHAPTER 23

SANTA INES

Nineteen Mission, founded September 17, 1804

A *fiesta* or party was about to begin to honor Saint Ines. It was for the saint for whom the mission was named. Everyone arose early. The church service was held. This marked the beginning of each day at the mission. Now the people gathered around to watch the games. The Indians played a game much like field hockey with a wooden ball. They raced against each other to see who could run the fastest. Bullfights brought crowds. At night everyone listened to musicians play in the mission orchestra. Laughing, singing, and music filled the air. Many people danced. Nobody worked that day.

The next morning work began as usual. The Indians could be proud of their work. They were good farmers. Their herds of cattle grew to 13,000 head. They learned many trades well. Their leather and iron crafts became famous. They carved designs in leather saddles.

Santa Ines became a school. Young pioneer men came here to study. This was the first college to be established in California.

The smooth running of the mission was stopped by the war with Spain in 1810. The soldiers did not get paid after that. They took out their anger on the Indians. The soldiers were called *leather jackets* because they wore heavy quilted hide coats. These protected them from the Indians' arrows. The soldiers also used rifles, swords, and hide shields for protection. Their weapons were much stronger weapons than those of the Indians.

When the earthquake of 1812 rocked the mission, the church was nearly destroyed. Other buildings fell down. Much time was spent rebuilding. A new and larger church was made of adobe and brick. Wood from pine trees nearby was used to build the walls stronger. A roof was made from tiles.

Trouble came on February 21, 1824. With little reason, a soldier harshly beat a young Indian man. The Indians became angry. They did not like this. Many other times the soldiers treated them roughly. The Indians set fire to the mission. They attacked the soldiers but left the padres alone.

This attack stirred the countryside! A few Indians rode to the nearby missions of La Purisima and Santa Barbara. They told others at these missions what had happened. The Indians at La Purisima and Santa Barbara decided to fight the soldiers too.

After the fighting ended, many Indians hid in the mountains. They joined the Tulare Indian tribe and lived among them. Only a few Indians returned.

The mission never became as successful as the padres had hoped. No more than 768 Indians ever lived here. It was a lonely place where few travelers visited.

Much later the mission buildings fell to ruin, though they were still used. Once a priest preaching from his pulpit (stand) felt it crumbling underneath him. It crashed to the ground. Though unhurt, he was very surprised.

128

TODAY AT THE MISSION

The Danish-American town of Solvang has grown up around this mission. Fine examples of mission arts and crafts can be seen here. Handmade leather seats, a copper bowl, objects in brass, gold, and silver are among the art treasures. Beautiful paintings hang in the church.

Many colorful flowers bloom all year. The garden is built in the shape of a cross. A water fountain sparkles in the center.

The top photograph shows the mission in earlier days and the bottom one, the mission as it looks today.

Mission San Rafael Arcangel during mission days

CHAPTER 24

SAN RAFAEL ARCANGEL

Twentieth Mission, founded December 14, 1817

San Rafael Arcangel was named for St. Raphael, the angel of healing. It started out as an *asistencia* or branch mission for Mission Dolores. It was established as a hospital branch where the sick Indians from Mission Dolores could come to get well.

Father Ramon Abella of Mission Dolores wrote a letter to Governor Sola for help. He told of the many Indians who were dying. They had caught "white men's sicknesses" like measles, chicken pox, and smallpox. The cold and rainy weather of San Francisco made other Indians sick.

The governor wrote back. What they needed was a warmer climate. The Indians could move to San Rafael. From the beginning, San Rafael was built to be simple not beautiful. One long building was built measuring about ninety feet long by forty feet wide. It was divided into many rooms including a hospital, living quarters, a storeroom, and a chapel (at one end). This mission was one of the few missions where no quadrangle was ever built.

Father Luis Gil knew something about medicine. He was chosen to head the new branch. Many Indians were cured under his care. The padre worked so hard to heal the Indians that his own health suffered. After two years, Father Gil was sent to another mission.

Father Juan Amoros, another priest, took over and taught the Indians trades. They learned to plant crops and care for animals. They became expert boatbuilders, blacksmiths, cowboys, carpenters, and weavers. The Indians worked hard to help the mission grow. Many Miwok Indians living on land nearby decided to come to live at the mission. What had started out as a hospital mission was now becoming more like other missions.

Father Amoros asked permission for San Rafael to become a full mission. On October 19, 1822, it was granted. Father Amoros guided the mission in its success. By 1828 1,140 Indians lived at the mission.

Though popular with the Indians, he did have trouble with an Indian named Chief Marin. He was a mission Indian who turned against the mission. Marin and another Indian, Quintin, caused trouble for the mission. Later Chief Marin came back to live there. Marin County is named for this Indian and the prison, San Quentin is named for his friend, Quintin.

The Indians at Mission San Rafael liked their lives and seemed happy. Another padre, Father Jose Mercado, came and changed that. He treated the Indians strictly and lost his temper often. He argued and caused trouble with the soldiers.

Once he feared Indians were planning to attack the mission. Giving the mission Indians guns, he sent them out to find the unfriendly Indians before they could attack. Many good Indians were needlessly killed in the battle. The church punished the padre for the harm he had done.

This became one of the first missions to be turned over to the Mexican government in 1833. General Mariano Vallejo was the leader who took over. He took many herds of animals and rich land for himself. This was land that by new law should have belonged to the Indians of the mission.

TODAY AT THE MISSION

The mission was finally abandoned in 1842 then sold for $8,000 in 1846. The weather crumbled and washed the mission buildings away. Now nothing is left of the old mission. A small replica of the mission chapel is built to remind visitors of mission days. In front of the chapel hang three of the four original bells. A star-shaped window is built to look like the one at the Carmel Mission. Attached to the chapel is a small wing that houses a gift shop with some mission objects. The church of St. Raphael stands next to the building in the city of San Rafael.

The rebuilt chapel at Mission San Rafael

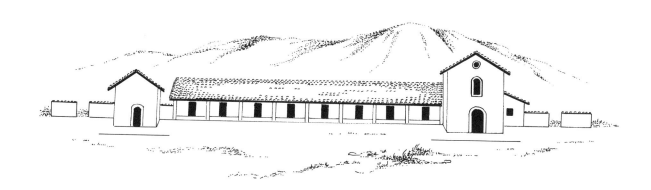

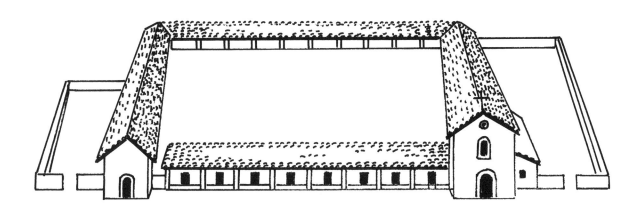

Mission San Francisco Solano Mission during mission days

134

CHAPTER 25

SAN FRANCISCO SOLANO

Twenty-first Mission, founded July 4, 1823

Russian fur trappers lived in northern California. They built Fort Ross at Bodega Bay. The Mexican government was against this. They wanted to stop Russia from taking over California. For this reason the last mission was founded close by. It is the only one to be built after Mexican Independence.

Father Jose Altimira wanted a mission of his own to run. He did not like his life at Mission Dolores. What could he do? He had been a priest only a few years. No one would listen to him. Then he came up with an idea.

He visited his friend, Governor Don Luis Arugello, in Monterey. Father Altimira suggested that missions Dolores and San Rafael be closed. Why not open a new mission in Sonoma to keep out the Russians? Governor Arugello liked Altimira's idea. The governor gave his permission. Altimira set out on his journey with a group of soldiers to find a place to build the new mission. He reached a beautiful valley that the Indians called the Valley of the Moon. The young padre chose the place for the mission.

Father Serria, who was President of the Missions, became angry. Who did Altimira think he was? Only the President of the Missions could decide to build a mission. Other priests were angry too. There was much quarreling about it. Finally, it was decided that missions Dolores and San Rafael and the new San Francisco Solano Mission would stay open.

Older missions usually gave animals and supplies to a new mission. Not much was given to this one because of hard feelings. Surprisingly, the Russians at Fort Ross gave them a small number of cattle.

Most of the adobe buildings were built the first year and a half. Everything was going well, though the padre complained. He thought the other padres talked against the mission. He was sure they discouraged Indians from coming here. Father Altimira was wrong. Many Indians did come. They came from San Rafael, Dolores, and San Jose Missions.

Few Indians wanted to stay. The priest caused trouble. He could have used kindness and love to teach them about religion and mission life. Instead, he punished them often.

The Indians became so unhappy that they attacked the mission and set fire to buildings. Afterwards, many Indians went back to their old missions. Some went to live in the mountains. The unhappy priest left too. He roamed from one mission to another, never staying long at any. Finally, he returned to Spain.

Another padre came to the mission. Father Buenaventura Fortuni was a good man who was friendly and kind. Many Indians came back to live at the mission. Local Indians from the Pomo and Coastal Miwok tribes came. Around 1830, almost 1,000 Indians lived at the mission. They were happy here for a short time longer.

After Mexican Independence, General Mariano Vallejo took over the mission. He divided the land among the Indians. Many turned it back to him in return for their care. The padres had made them too dependent on the mission system. With the padres gone, no one was left to look out for them.

Through the years, the mission was used for many things. It became a blacksmith shop and later a saloon. It was also used as a barn for animals and a storeroom for hay.

Mission San Francisco de Solano in ruins

TODAY AT THE MISSION

This mission is one of the two owned by the State of California. Most of the buildings lay in ruins until the Historic Landmark League took over. They began to rebuild it in 1903. The chapel and the padre's living quarters can be seen today. A small museum is housed in the padre's quarters.

Beautiful watercolor paintings by Chris Jorgensen hang inside the mission. He traveled up the coast of California visiting the missions in the early days by wagon. He studied and painted them for many years.

Located in Sonoma, the mission is in the heart of the wine-growing area of California. Did you realize that the first people to plant the vines were the padres? Now every year the blessing of the grapes is celebrated at the mission as part of the Vintage Festival usually held in September.

The mission is part of the Sonoma State Historic Park. A trip to this mission and its surrounding buildings is a fascinating walk through history. The Sonoma Barracks, the Plaza, La Casa Grande, the Blue Wing Inn, and the Toscano Hotel will be remembered for their importance in early California.

The mission today

CHAPTER 26

ASISTENCIAS: THE LITTLE MISSIONS

Pala Asistencia after mission days

Besides the missions, the Indians built *asistencias*. An *asistencia* is a branch mission belonging to a larger *mother* mission. Some *asistencias* consisted of only chapels. Other *asistencias* looked like small missions with buildings for the padre and Indians to live and work in. Sometimes the padre lived there all the time. Other times he would travel from the larger mission to give church services.

Why were *asistencias* needed? The missions were built along the coast of California. Many Indians lived in the mountains or far from the ocean. The padres wanted to teach them about Christianity too.

139

Padre Payeras, who served as President of the Missions at one time, came up with a plan. Why not build a second group of missions further in from the ocean? They could be built near where these Indians lived. The governor turned the plan down. Over many years, these smaller *asistencias* were built instead. It was hoped by the padres that one day they would become full missions.

One of the most important *asistencias* was San Antonio de Pala. The story of this *asistencia* began when Father Juan Mariner came looking for land. He wanted to find a good spot for a new mission. In August, 1795, he came to the Pala Valley. He liked the beautiful land and the river flowing through it. The bright, friendly Indians welcomed him. He wanted the San Luis Rey de Francia Mission to be built here. Others wanted it to be built closer to the ocean. When it was, this land was forgotten for a while.

Father Peyri at Mission San Luis Rey tried to interest these Indians in Christianity. He invited them to come to live at the mission. They liked living in their beautiful valley and did not want to leave it. Still, they seemed interested in the new religion. The padre chose the land to build an *asistencia* on June 13, 1816. It was founded as a branch of Mission San Luis Rey.

It took several years to build the buildings. The padre showed the Indians how to make thousands of adobe bricks and tiles. They cut down cedar trees growing nearby for roof beams. With horses and oxen, they carried them to the mission.

They built a chapel long and narrow. Inside they laid tiles for the floor and painted the walls. A bell tower was built apart from the other buildings. Rocks from the river were used for a base. Most of the tower was made out of adobe bricks fifty feet tall. Two bells were hung in it.

There are two stories told about it. One is about a bird that landed on the cross as Father Peyri put it on top of the tower. The bird was so happy it started to sing and dropped a cactus seed from its mouth. The seed sprouted and a cactus grew.

The other story is about Father Peyri climbing the tower. He planted a cactus at the foot of the cross. It served as a symbol of Chrisitianity coming to the wild lands.

When they were finished building it, the *asistencia* looked like a small mission. There were rooms for the padres and Indians, storehouses, a granary, and fences for the animals. The Indians also built a water channel.

Fewer Indians came here than that of major missions. Still, the herds of animals grew. The Indians planted crops of wheat, corn, beans, and other plants to eat. Most of the grain for the larger mission was grown here. They planted a vineyard for grapes and an orchard with fruit and olive trees. Soon more Indians came. After a few years, over a thousand Indians had become Christians.

Why were so many of these Indians interested in the new religion? Their own religion was like the Christian religion in some ways. They believed in one god. They believed in a future life after death. They celebrated with many ceremonies in this religion too. For some of these reasons, they accepted Christianity easier than some of the other California tribes.

The *asistencia* progressed well until secularization came in 1834. This meant the Mexican government replaced the padres with administrators to run the missions. Mission San Luis Rey had trouble. Government leaders wanted the fine land for their own.

On August 22, 1835, Mission San Luis Rey and this *asistencia* were taken over by Pio Pico and Pablo de la Portilla. Pico ran it badly, and the Indians suffered. He sold it to Antonio J. Cot and Jose A. Pico on May 18, 1846. They paid $2,000 in silver and $437.50 in wheat. The sale was against the law.

Missionary padres did not live here after this. They still came once in a while to hold church services.

TODAY AT THE ASISTENCIA

San Antonio de Pala looks much like it did in the early days. Buildings have been rebuilt. Bells in the bell tower are still rung to call the Indians to church. This is the only church in the mission chain still used for services by the Indians. The bell tower is famous.

141

The museum has many interesting objects. There are woven baskets and pottery made by the Indians. Several statues can be seen. The statue of San Luis Rey is here. This and the one of Mother Mary were created by Mexican artists. Statues of St. Anthony and St. Dominc were created by Indian artists.

There is an Indian reservation nearby of Palatingua Indians. These are a different tribe from the Shoshonean Indians of mission days. Each year the Corpus Christi Fiesta is given. It is a celebration of God's love for man. Since 1816, not one year has been missed in celebrating this fiesta.

Because of the interest in this *asistencia* over the years, it has now become a full mission. Many do not count it among the list of missions since it became one after mission days.

OTHER ASISTENCIAS

Many of the *asistencias* have been destroyed. In the early days they were built as they were needed. Among them were Santa Ysabel, San Bernardino, Santa Margarita, Las Flores Nuestra Senora La Reina de Los Angeles, San Miguel, San Miguelito, Mesa Grande, and Santa Ysabel.

CHAPTER 27

THE END OF THE MISSIONS

"War! War!" cried the messenger. "Mexico is at war!" The news was shouted all over California. Mexico had declared their independence from Spain. They wanted to rule themselves. They grew tired of the King of Spain telling them what to do. The battle called the Hildago Revolt broke out in 1810. Suddenly, all supplies were cut off to the missions. During the war, they could not trade with other countries or Mexico for what they needed. The government ordered the missions to support the soldiers and their families. The government no longer had money to pay the soldiers.

More shoes, more blankets, and more food. The demands of the soldiers never ended. They would not work. The mission would have to take care of them. The padres wrote letters to the government. They told how unfair this was to the Indians and the missions. Their letters did not do any good.

The soldiers had always caused trouble. Not many people at first wanted to come to California from Mexico. Some of them had been criminals back in Mexico. They came to guard and protect the missions. They fought with the Indians. Often they argued with the padres and would not follow orders.

For years the missions went on like this. The heavy load of supporting the soldiers discouraged the Indians. Soon supplies disappeared and people went hungry. Life was difficult for the Indians.

"Mexico has won the war!" was the excited cry. Mexico won their independence from Spain in 1821. This was not good news to the missions. Life did not get any better. Leaders in the Mexican government looked at the rich lands of the missions with greedy thoughts. They wanted to get rid of the padres and missions. They wanted to take the land. They passed many laws to make this come true.

They made the padres sign a paper called "an oath of loyalty." It said they would obey the new Mexican government. The padres were Spanish citizens. Many felt loyal to Spain and would not sign the paper. The leaders became angry. They passed another law to make Spaniards under the age of 60 leave the country. This meant most of the padres were forced to leave.

The Indians became Mexican citizens. They could vote now, but few were given the chance. Many grew tired of strict mission life. In later years they had enjoyed little freedom. Many had run away, but now even more left.

Mexican leaders came to rule the missions after the padres left. The land belonged to the Indians. It was supposed to be divided among them. Settlers and leaders took most of it instead. Governor Pio Pico sold many of the missions, though it was against the law.

What was left for the Indians? The Spaniards had come and taken their land and changed their lives. Few Indians had been taught to read and write. They had spent their time working at useful trades for the good of the missions. They did not have much practice in governing themselves. The padres had made them too dependent. Many knew no other life than mission life. What did they know of living off the land? Their people had left that life many years before. But some did try to go back to the mountains and live in the old ways. Others went to work on newly-formed ranches or stayed on at missions until they were forced to leave.

The mission system that had begun in 1769, ended about 70 years later. It had lasted about as long as one person's lifetime. In that time, it had changed the lives of the Indians forever.

CHAPTER 28

FATHER JUNIPERO SERRA

Founder of the Missions

On November 21, 1713, Miguel Jose Serra was born. He grew up in the small village of Petra on the island of Majorca in Spain.

His parents were named Antonio and Margarita. They were poor people who worked hard but could not read or write. In their home, there was much love and kindness for Miguel and his sister, Juana.

As a boy, Miguel was shy and sickly. Sometimes he was not strong enough to play with the other children. His life became centered around the Catholic church. His faith in God grew strong. He sang in the choir and learned his lessons well.

As he grew older, Miguel decided to become a Franciscan priest. At first the school turned him down. Those who knew him told them what a good priest Miguel would make.

When he became a priest, he changed his name to Junipero Serra. At the same time, he also became a teacher. He taught classes at the University of Majorca for seven years. The students liked him, and he could have spent the rest of his life teaching.

But his dream was to become a missionary. A missionary is a religious person who wants to travel to other countries and tell those people about God. When he heard missionaries were needed in Mexico, he told them he wished to go. First, he was sent to San Fernando College to a school for missionaries. After this, he was given charge of five missions already built. He went to live in the Sierra Gorda Mountains of Mexico. Here he worked for nine years teaching the Indians Christianity. These were happy years for Father Serra.

Next, the church wanted him to become a traveling missionary. He was to preach all over Mexico wherever he was needed. He did this for eight years. Sometimes it was dangerous. His travels took him to mining camps and seaports. They took him along jungle rivers where deadly snakes hung from trees overhead. Often he spent the night where fierce, wild animals roamed. But Father Serra was a brave man.

The church leader knew this. When missions were to be established in California, Father Serra was chosen to be President. He was 55 years old by then. Bravely, he set out to found the first nine of twenty-one missions.

Believing strongly in the mission system, he walked many miles by foot to found new missions. He traveled to check on old ones. His many journeys caused him to limp. Often when he was sick, he would travel anyway. Finally on August 28, 1784, he died of a sickness called tuberculosis. He was seventy-one years old. He had served his church as a missionary for thirty-five years.

DATES IN CALIFORNIA MISSION HISTORY

1542- Juan Cabrillo discovers San Diego and claims California for Spain.

1579- Sir Francis Drake claims California for England.

1602- Discovery of Monterey Bay by Sebastian Vizcaino for Spain.

1768- King Charles III of Spain ordered colonization of California to begin.

1769- Sea and land expeditions set out for California.

July 16, 1769- Mission San Diego de Alcala founded.

June 3, 1770- Mission San Carlos Borromeo (Carmel) founded.

July 14, 1771- Mission San Antonio de Padua founded.

September 8, 1771- Mission San Gabriel Arcangel founded.

September 1, 1772- Mission San Luis Obispo founded.

June 29, 1776- Mission San Francisco de Asis (Dolores) founded.

November 5, 1775- Mission San Diego attacked by Indians.

November 1, 1776- Mission San Juan Capistrano founded.

January 12, 1777- Mission Santa Clara de Asis founded.

March 31, 1782- Mission San Buenaventura founded.

August 28, 1784- Death of Father Junipero Serra.

December 4, 1786- Mission Santa Barbara founded.

December 8, 1787- Mission La Purisima Concepcion founded.

August 28, 1791- Mission Santa Cruz founded.

October 9, 1791- Mission Nuestra Senora de la Soledad founded.

June 11, 1797- Mission San Jose founded.

June 24, 1797- Mission San Juan Bautista founded.

July 25, 1797- Mission San Miguel Arcangel founded.

September 8, 1797- Mission San Fernando Rey founded.

June 13, 1789- Mission San Luis Rey de Francia founded.

September 17, 1804- Mission Santa Ines founded.

December 14, 1817- Mission San Rafael Arcangel founded.

July 4, 1823- Mission San Francisco Solano founded.

September 16, 1821- Mexican Independence from Spain.

1833 - Secularization law passed.

Feburary 21, 1824- Indian revolt at Santa Ines Mission.

1846-1848- Mexican War with the United States.

February, 1848- California becomes a United States territory.

CALIFORNIA MISSIONS AND THEIR LOCATIONS

Mission San Diego de Alcala
10818 San Diego Mission Rd.
San Diego, CA 92108
(619) 281-8449

Mission San Antonio de Padua
Hunter Liggett Milt. Reservation
P.O. Box 803
Jolon, CA 93928
(408) 385-4478

Mission San Gabriel Arcangel
567 West Mission Dr.
San Gabriel, CA 91776
(818) 282-5191

Mission San Luis Obispo de Tolosa
941 Chorro St.
San Luis Obispo, CA 93402
(805) 543-1034

Mission San Francisco de Asis
3321 16th St.
San Francisco, CA 94114
(415) 621-8203

Mission San Juan Capistrano
Camino Capistrano / P.O. Box 697
San Juan Capistrano, CA 92693
(714) 493-1111

Mission Santa Clara de Asis
University of Santa Clara
820 Alviso St./ P.O. Box 178
Santa Clara, CA 95052
(408) 296-4656

Mission San Carlos Borromeo
3080 Rio Road/ P.O. Box 2235
Carmel, CA 93921
(408) 264-1271

Mission La Purisima Concepcion
Purisima & Mission Gate Rd.
RFD#102
Lompoc, CA 93436
(805) 733-3713

Mission Santa Barbara
2201 Laguna St.
Santa Barbara, CA 93105
(805) 682-4713

Mission Santa Cruz
126 High St.
Santa Cruz, CA 95060
(408) 426-5686

Mission Santa Ines
1760 Mission Dr.\P.O. Box 408
Solvang, CA 93463
(805) 688-4815

Mission San Rafael Arcangel
1104 5th St.
San Rafael, CA 94901
(415) 456-3016

Mission San Francisco Solano
114 East Spain St.
P.O. Box 167
Sonoma, CA 95476
(707) 938-1519

Mission San Buenaventura
211 East Main St.
Ventura, CA 93001
(805) 643-4318

Mission Nuestra Senora de la Soledad
c/o Our Lady of Soledad Parish
36641 Fort Romie Rd. /P.O. Box 506
Soledad, CA 93960
(408) 678-2586

Mission San Juan Bautista
San Juan Bautista St. Hist. Plaza
408 S. Second St.
San Juan Bautista, CA 95045
(408) 623-2127

Mission San Fernando Rey de Espana
15151 Mission Blvd.
San Fernando, CA 91435
(818) 361-0186

Mission San Luis Rey de Francia
4050 Mission Blvd.
San Luis Rey, CA 92068
(619) 757-3651

Mission San Jose
43300 Mission Blvd.
Fremont, CA 94539
(415) 657-1797

Mission San Miguel Arcangel
700 Mission St.
P.O. Box 69
San Miguel, CA 93451
(805) 467-3256

MUSEUMS OF INTEREST

Albinger Archaeological Museum
113 East Main St.
Ventura, CA 93001

California State Indian Museum
2618 K Street
Sacramento, CA 94816

De Saisset Museum
University of Santa Clara
820 Alviso St.
Santa Clara, CA 95053

The Junipero Serra Museum
2727 Presidio Dr.
San Diego, CA 92138

Lompoc Museum
200 South H St.
Lompoc, CA 93436

Santa Barbara Presidio
123 East Canon Peridido
Santa Barbara, CA 93102

Ventura County Historical Museum
100 East Main St.
Ventura, CA 93001

GLOSSARY

adobe sun-dried bricks made of clay earth, straw, and water

alcalde Indian leader elected by his people at the mission

altar a table used by religious people in church services

arrowhead the pointed tip of an arrow made of stone or metal

asistencia small mission or sub-mission

atole a mush made of cornmeal

baptism religious ceremony given for a person to become a Christian

barracks rooms for the soldiers to live

blacksmith a person who makes objects out of iron

carpenter a person who makes objects out of wood

carreta wooden cart used to carry heavy objects

ceremony ritual

chapel small church

community a group of people living in the same area

convent a church and building for religious women to live

convento building for the priests' rooms

design drawing

dialects different ways of saying the same language

excavation digging in the earth to find the remains from another time

expedition a group of people taking a long trip to a faraway place

fiesta a party or celebration

governor a leader who rules a country or territory

granary rooms for storing grain

gristmill a mill used to grind grain

kiln a brick oven used to bake adobe bricks

loom a machine used to weave cloth

medicine man or woman a person called on to heal the sick

mano a stone used to mash meal

metate a stone or volanic slab used for grinding corn or wheat

miracle an event that cannot be explained

missionary religious person who travels to tell people about God

padre Spanish name for priest, a religious person in some churches

planks wooden boards

pozole a stew of vegetables and beef

presidio fort

pueblo town

quadrangle mission buildings built in a four-sided shape

reata leather rope used by Indian cowboys

regiodore Indian leader elected to help the alcalde

restoration repair to original condition

saint a person who is considered holy by the church

saloon a bar

sandstone yellow stone used to build some of mission churches

secularization Mexican laws that took the missions away from the church and gave them to the government

settle to come to live

shield an object designed to protect a person

siesta Spanish word for rest

stable a building where horses are kept

tallow animal fat used to make soap and candles

tanner a person who tans animal hides

tattoo to mark or decorate the skin

territory land

tile piece of clay baked in kiln, often used for roofs

trade exchanging one object for another or a type of skilled work

tribe a group of people who share the same language and culture

vat pit

viceroy a leader who rules a country for the king

village a small group of houses

water channel a system of water pipes

BIBLIOGRAPHY : BOOKS

Ainsworth, Katherine and Edward. *In the Shade of the Juniper Tree: A Life of Fray Junipero Serra*, Doubleday, 1970.

Bauer, Helen. *California Indian Days*, Doubleday, 1968.

Bauer, Helen. *California Mission Days,* Doubleday, 1951.

Bleeker, Sonia. *The Mission Indians of California,* Morrow, 1956.

Brown, Karl F. *California Missions: a Guide to the Historic Trails of the Padres,* Garden City Publishing Co., Inc., 1939.

Carillo, J.M. *The Story of Mission San Antonio de Pala*, Paisano Press, 1959.

Englehardt, Fray Zephryrin. *Mission Nuestra Senora de la Soledad,* Mission Santa Barbara, 1929.

—-*Mission San Carlos Borromeo (Carmelo)*, Mission Santa Barbara, 1934.

—-*Mission San Juan Bautista*, Mission Santa Barbara, 1931.

—-*Mission San Luis Obispo*, Mission Santa Barbara, 1933.

—-*Mission Santa Ines*, Mission Santa Barbara, 1932.

—-*San Antonio de Padua*, Ballena Press, 1929.

—-*San Buenaventura*, Mission Santa Barbara, 1930.

—-*San Diego Mission*, The Janes Barry Co., 1920.

—-*San Fernando Rey,* Franciscan Herald Press, 1927.

—-*San Francisco or Mission Dolores,* Franciscan Herald Press, 1924.

—-*San Gabriel Mission and the Beginning of Los Angeles*, Mission San Gabriel, 1927.

Engelhardt, Fray Zephryin. *San Juan Capistrano Mission,* Standard Printing Co., 1922.

—-*San Luis Rey Mission*, The James Barry Co., 1921.

—-*San Miguel Arcangel*, Mission Santa Barbara, 1929.

—-*Santa Barbara Mission*, The James Barry Co., 1923.

Foster, Lee. *The Beautiful California Missions*, Beautiful America Publishing Co., 1977.

Goodman, Marian. *Missions of California*, Redwood City Tribune, 1962.

Hawthorne, Hildegarde. *California's Missions — Their Romance and Beauty*, Appleton-Century Co., Inc., 1942.

Heizer, Robert and Elsasser, Albert. *The Natural World of the California Indians,* University of California Press, 1980.

James, George Wharton. *In and Out of the Old Missions of California*, Little, Brown & Co., 1905.

Kocher, Paul. *California's Old Missions: The Story of the Founding of the 21* Franciscan Missions in Spanish Alta California 1769-1823, Franciscan Herald Press, 1976.

Older, Ms. Fremont. *California Missions and Their Romances,* Tudor Publish
ing Co., 1945.

Roberts, Helen M. *Mission Tales,* Pacific Books, Publishers, 1948.

Smilie, Robert S. *The Sonoma Mission: San Francisco Solano de Sonoma,*
Valley Publishers, 1975.

Sunset. *The California Missions: a Pictorial History,* Lane Book Co., 1974.

Tompkins, Walker. *Old Spanish Santa Barbara,* McNally & Loftin Publishers,
1967.

Torchiana, H.V. Van Coenen. *Story of the Mission Santa Cruz,* Paul Elder &
Co., 1933.

Webb, Edith. *Indian Life at the Old Missions,* University of Nebraska Press,
1952.

Young, Stanley. *The Missions of California,* Chronicle Books, 1988.

Ziebold, Edna. *Indians of Early Southern California,* Perc Sapsis Publisher,
1969.

BIBLIOGRAPHY: PAMPHLETS

Earnest, Aileen Ryan. "Mission Vestments," 1975.

Engbeck, Joseph H., Jr. "La Purisima Mission State Historic Park," State of
California.

Geiger, Maynard. "Father Junipero Serra Paintings," Franciscan Frs., 1958.

‑‑"The Indians of Mission Santa Barbara in Paganism and Christianity,"
Franciscan Fathers, 1960.

Gordon, Dudley. "Junipero Serra: California's First Citizen," Cultural Assets
Press, 1969.

Harrington, Marie. "Mission San Fernando: a Guide," San Fernando Valley
Historical Society, Inc., 1971.

Kochner, Paul H. "Mission San Luis Obispo de Tolosa; a Historical Sketch,"
Blake Printing & Publishing, 1972.

McIntyre, Francis "Padre Junipero Serra and the California Missions," 1949.

Morrison, Col. E.G. Morie. "Sonoma, California's Mission San Francisco
Solano," Mission Sesquicentennial Commission, 1973.

Mylar, Isacc . "Early Days at the Mission San Juan Bautista," Valley Publish
ers, 1976.

Ray, Sister Mary Dominic and Engbeck, Joseph H., Jr. "Gloria Dei: The Story
of California Mission Music," State of California.

Tac, Pablo; edited and translated by Hewes, Gordon and Minna. "Indian Life
at Mission San Luis Rey," Old Mission, 1958.

INDEX

ABOUT THE AUTHOR

Linda Lyngheim is a California history enthusiast. She has written two other books for children on California history, *Gold Rush Adventure* and *Father Junipero Serra the Traveling Missionary*. Writing for adults, she has authored non-fiction books and magazine articles. She received her Bachelor of Arts degree in social science from California State University, Fresno and an M.L.S. degree in library science from University of Southern California. As a librarian, she has worked for the Glendale Public Library and the Los Angeles Public Library. She resides in Los Angeles.

ABOUT THE ILLUSTRATOR

Phyllis Garber is a graduate of Carnegie Mellon University. She studied at the Pittsburgh Art Institute and Pasadena School of Art. This is the third book she has illustrated for children. As a painter, she has received many local art awards for her watercolors. She resides in Laguna Niguel.